PHILIP DEAN was born in Queensland and is a graduate of the Queensland College of Art and the University of Queensland. His writing for the theatre includes *Tall Green Stranger in a Ceramic Pot* (for the Princess Theatre, 1994); *Long Gone Lonesome Cowgirls* (for La Boite Theatre, 1995), which subsequently toured Australia and was adapted for ABC Radio; *Biting Pavlov* (for Pandemonium at the Warren Street Theatre, 1996); *Family Values* and *Down and Out in Paradise* (for Rolling Jaffa under the title *Disconnected*, 1998); and *First Asylum* (for La Boite Theatre, 1999). He received a Matilda Award in 1995. He currently lives in Brisbane.

AFTER JANUARY

Adapted by Philip Dean

from the novel by Nick Earls

Currency Press • Sydney

First published in 2000 by
Currency Press Ltd,
PO Box 2287, Strawberry Hills NSW 2012
enquiries@currency.com.au; www.currency.com.au
in association with
La Boite Theatre, Brisbane

This revised edition published 2000

Reprinted 2003, 2006, 2008, 2015, 2017.

NATIONAL LIBRARY OF AUSTRALIA CIP DATA
Dean, Philip, 1954–.

    After January.
    Rev ed.
    ISBN 978 0 86819 636 7.
    1. Interpersonal relations—Drama. 2. Surfing—Drama. 3. Love—Drama. I. Earls, Nick, 1963– After January. II. Title.
A822.3

Typeset by Dean Nottle
Cover design by Sasha Middleton, ToadShow.

Currency Press acknowledges the Traditional Owners of the Country on which we live and work. We pay our respects to all Aboriginal and Torres Strait Islander Elders, past and present.

Contents

PLAYWRIGHT'S NOTE

When I was approached to adapt *After January*, I confess I had not read any of Nick Earls' novels. So I began as a reader, turning the pages and delighting in the stories. I loved their vivid sense of place, and especially that the place was familiar; that the beaches, streets and cafes were a part of my life and its private stories. It's easy to feel that the centre of the world is New York or London or even Sydney, when in fact the world has no centre and everywhere is far away and exotic to somewhere. I also liked the sense that ordinary lives and small events were worth writing about. In putting those lives on the stage there are, and must be, many changes and shifts of emphasis. And while each work has to stand on its own merits, I hope that those who have already enjoyed the novel will find some of the same humour and tenderness in the play, and that those who have not will be motivated to do so.

Philip Dean
Brisbane, January 2000

After January was first produced by La Boite Theatre, Brisbane, on 24 February 2000, with the following cast:

ALEX	Yalin Ozucelik
TESSA / GAIL	Queenie van de Zandt
LEN / CLIFF / FRED	Jack Heywood
FORTUNA	Kylie Morris

Director, Lewis Jones
Designer, Kate Stewart
Lighting, Andrew Meadows
Sound Designer, Campbell Misfeld
Stage Manager, Tiffany Noack
Assistant Director, Jennifer Boyle

Characters

ALEX, 17
FORTUNA, 17
TESSA, Alex's mother, about 40
CLIFF, Fortuna's father, about 45
GAIL, Fortuna's mother, about 40
LEN, neighbour, about 60
FRED BRAHAMS, plumber

The parts of TESSA and GAIL can be played by the same
  actor.
The parts of CLIFF, LEN and FRED can be played by the
  same actor.

We hear Frente's 'Accidentally Kelly Street' playing as the lights come up on a beach house in Caloundra. It is morning. There are two stools beside a kitchen bench and a bean bag on the floor. On the bench are a phone, kettle, toaster, portable CD player, plates, cups, etc. ALEX is reading the paper. TESSA enters and turns down the music. She feels the kettle and begins to make coffee.

TESSA   Anything in the paper?

ALEX   Not really.

TESSA   You're not worrying about it, are you?

ALEX   No, it's a few weeks away. A couple of weeks. [*Pause.*] Eighteen days.

TESSA   A tertiary offer is no reflection of a person's worth. You do realise that, don't you?

ALEX   Yes, Mum.

TESSA   And whatever you get, even if it's not law, you'll have a great time.

ALEX   I know.

TESSA smiles. It's obvious that they have had this conversation before. She sits on a stool and opens a book.

ALEX   [*to the audience*] Today neither of us want to have this conversation. I would be told again about her days at uni, the great times she had, the late nights, the medical student practical jokes. And so on. This is supposed to help me. But what if it doesn't work out this way? It seems distinctly possible that the cool people will find each other early and I'll be left with the losers. With the people who never miss a lecture, never go out at night and bring packed lunches. Perhaps I should tell her now and lessen the inevitable pain.

TESSA So. Good holiday then?

ALEX Yeah, fine. Fine. What about you?

TESSA Great. Perfect. Very relaxing. What will you do today, watch the cricket?

ALEX It's a rest day.

TESSA Six extra hours to kill. It's not easy in Caloundra.

ALEX I'll swim, sleep, go to the library.

TESSA A perfect lazy day then.

ALEX Perfect.

TESSA Do you want any of your friends to come up?

ALEX I think they're all doing other things at the moment. We'll be back in Brisbane soon, anyway.

TESSA That's right. This all comes to an end, doesn't it? Back to Brisbane, back to work. What are you going to do when I'm back at work?

ALEX Watch cricket I suppose. So it'll be exactly the same as here, except the TV'll be bigger.

LEN enters. He is about sixty and wears a bright Hawaiian shirt.

LEN   G'day young Alex. Fancy a frame or two?

He mimes a pool shot.

ALEX   That'd be good.

LEN   When you're ready.

LEN *leaves.* TESSA *returns to her book.* ALEX *picks up a bright red bike helmet.*

ALEX   [*to the audience*] My bike helmet. Chosen by my parents so I can efficiently signal the danger I represent. It's hot on the road and whatever I'm signalling I don't think it's danger. The library, though, is air-conditioned. And who knows what might happen there? [*He puts on the helmet.*] I have this fantasy of bumping into someone young, female and desirable in any public place. This afternoon, for instance, among the fiction shelves. Striking up a conversation. Revealing myself to be clever, funny and equally desirable... even though I've forgotten to take off the bike helmet and look like a cross between a Redhead match and a complete dickhead.

TESSA   [*looking up from her book*] It's a body you'll grow into.

ALEX   Thanks Mum.

TESSA   What about that girl Juliet, the one who was in the play with you?

ALEX *removes the helmet.*

ALEX   [*to the audience*] We kissed in the school play and it all lingers in my mind like a relationship. Afterwards I wrote a story when she was all I could think about. I showed it to my mother in a moment of weakness.

TESSA   It's beautiful. It's beautiful, and nobody dies. There's no blood in it at all. No weapons, no heavy machinery, no mutilation. It's so unlike you. I'm going to make some copies.

ALEX *relives the embarrassment.*

ALEX   [*to the audience*] It ended up in the school magazine and won the literary competition and gave me a fleeting kind of fame. I don't know if Juliet saw it. I haven't seen her since. [*Pause.*] A year ago my mother looked at me across the breakfast table.

TESSA   I've thought about it and I want you to know that if you told me you were gay I could come to terms with it.

ALEX   [*to the audience*] My mother who works at uni as a doctor and who likes to be in touch with youth. Who, I suspect, secretly extends her definition of youth a year with each birthday. But perhaps I'm not being fair. She hasn't had her nose pierced, or experimented with grunge, and she will still argue with anybody that Fleetwood Mac's 'Rumors' is one of the top ten records of all time.

TESSA   You going for a swim?

ALEX   Yeah.

TESSA   I might take my book back to bed. Make the most of my last week of holidays.

TESSA *wanders off.*

ALEX   [*to the audience*] I go to the beach early because I'm in the habit of it. Towel, seventy cents for the paper from the Big Pineapple ashtray, surf.

As he speaks he collects his towel and coins and moves to the beach where he towels himself dry.

ALEX   My brain doesn't work 'till it's woken by the surf, so I need a routine. This, my mother says, is a habit of my father's, and hence not highly regarded. [*He stares out to sea.*] On the water there's a girl, legs balanced perfectly and comfortably on the board, sun-bleached hair in a wet ponytail. And the sun is partly behind her, reflecting off the water so I can't see her well. [*He blinks, then looks away.*] I buy the paper from the newsagent in Seaview Terrace on the way home.

He moves towards the house. LEN *enters holding a sheet of paper.*

LEN   Now, young Alex, you've got a bit of an interest in poetry.

ALEX   I'll have breakfast and come over.

LEN   When you're ready.

LEN *leaves.* ALEX *moves into the house and gets himself some breakfast.*

ALEX [*to the audience*] It's as though I'm passing through this summer in a bubble. Vaguely detached and drifting. [*Pause.*] I talk to myself often when I'm alone. In a normal conversational voice. Sometimes I even interview myself, as though I've become famous for something. I did quite a few interviews after the Juliet story. Magazines, 'Creatures of the Spotlight' on Triple J. Instead of studying I was telling the chemistry textbook how I was handling being in the public eye. Sure it takes away some of your privacy, I told it, but that's the price you have to pay. All this in my room, by myself, sitting at my desk at night with the bedroom door open.

TESSA *enters.*

TESSA I went to an Adolescent Medicine seminar today and one of the speakers said that if your adolescent child is alone in their room with the door shut they're almost certainly masturbating.

TESSA *leaves.*

ALEX Always with the door open.

He moves to the beach.

ALEX Notes for 'The Poem About the Watcher'.
So I am the watcher now.
And she is perfect form.
And she moves with the grace of a dolphin.
As though there are no angles, only curves, arcs, circles.

About this I can write a poem. And show it to no one. [*Pause.* ALEX *grins at the audience, slightly embarrassed.*] At first the surf was mine this morning. But more people are arriving now, crowding the water.

He stands, shakes out the towel and rattles the coins in his hand. From offstage we hear a car start and a terrible crunching of gears and then silence.

ALEX   Shower, newspaper, breakfast.

FORTUNA *enters, searching through her bag and obviously unimpressed. She is tanned, wears a T-shirt over her togs, has long hair in a ponytail and a nose ring. She removes the towel from around her waist, lays it on the sand and empties out the contents of her bag. There isn't much: a brush, suncream, sunglasses. She is looking for coins but finds only a five-cent piece. She doesn't notice* ALEX.

ALEX   Is there anything I can do?

FORTUNA *doesn't hear him.*

ALEX   [*aside*] This is a mistake and I'm about to make a dickhead of myself. [*To* FORTUNA] Do you have a problem? [*Aside*] Other than this pathetic nerd performing an unnoticed act of significant foolhardiness. [*To* FORTUNA] Is there anything I can do?

FORTUNA *looks at him and frowns.*

FORTUNA   [*pointing*] My Moke... I think it's the clutch cable.

ALEX	So what are you going to do?
FORTUNA	I think it's just disconnected.
ALEX	Right.
FORTUNA	So it needs to be reconnected.
ALEX	Yeah. How would you reconnect it?
FORTUNA	Do you have any tools? Screwdriver? Wrench?
ALEX	Not on me, no.
FORTUNA	Anywhere nearby?
ALEX	I live nearby, and there might be tools, but I really don't know much about engines.
FORTUNA	So when you offered to do something, what did you have in mind?
ALEX	I don't know, a push start maybe. But that probably wouldn't be much use, would it?
FORTUNA	No.
ALEX	Right.
FORTUNA	So I'll have to call my father. Do you have any change you could lend me for the call?
ALEX	Um, no. You can phone from my house if you like. The white house through the trees.
FORTUNA	Okay.

They move to the beach house. ALEX *indicates the phone.*

ALEX	My mother's asleep.

While FORTUNA *speaks on the phone* ALEX *switches on the kettle and puts bread in the toaster.*

FORTUNA	[*on the phone*] It's me... At Caloundra. The clutch cable's come off again... I don't

know... The carpark at Moffet's Beach... That's okay. Bye. [*She hangs up.*] My father will be a while. He's tied up. Something he can't leave. So I guess I should go back to the car and wait for him there.

ALEX   You can wait here if you want.

FORTUNA   Okay, thanks.

ALEX   You can probably see the car from the veranda.

FORTUNA   Do you live here?

ALEX   It's a holiday house. My parents own it. So I'm here every summer. What about you?

FORTUNA   I live here. Well not exactly here. Little Mountain, just inland. With my family.

ALEX   What would you like, tea or coffee?

FORTUNA   What kind of tea do you have?

ALEX   Bags.

FORTUNA   Yeah, but what kind of tea is in the bags?

ALEX   Oh, right.

He passes her a tin of assorted tea bags.

ALEX   How long have you lived at the coast?

FORTUNA   A couple of years. We've moved around a bit. It's good here though, I suppose. We used to be up north.

ALEX   We come here every summer. I live in Brisbane the rest of the time.

FORTUNA *smiles.* ALEX *tries to think of something to say.*

ALEX   Do you surf here much?

FORTUNA No. I surf where the waves are, and they're not usually good here. They've been okay the last couple of days.

ALEX It hasn't been a good summer for waves.

FORTUNA Have you got a board?

ALEX No. I've got a ski, but I usually body surf.

FORTUNA Body surf.

ALEX *realises how uncool body surfers are in the eyes of board riders.*

ALEX Have some more toast.

FORTUNA *indicates the jar of honey.*

FORTUNA I know these people. It's good honey. Second best on the coast.

ALEX Second best?

FORTUNA This is good bread, too. Who made it?

ALEX Coles, I think.

FORTUNA Really? My father makes our bread. [*Pause.*] So what do you do in Brisbane? School?

ALEX Well, not anymore.

FORTUNA You've finished?

ALEX Yeah, just finished.

FORTUNA Me too.

ALEX Waiting to see what I get.

FORTUNA Your offer?

ALEX Yeah.

FORTUNA When is that? Soon?

ALEX About sixteen days.

FORTUNA *About* sixteen days.

ALEX   Yes.

FORTUNA   Sixteen days and counting.

ALEX   I just happened to know the date.

FORTUNA   You knew it was exactly sixteen days.

ALEX   Okay, so I'm waiting.

FORTUNA   What are you waiting for?

ALEX   Arts-Law. Queensland Uni.

FORTUNA   What made you pick Arts-Law?

ALEX   I don't know. There were lots of things I knew I'd hate. That wasn't one of them. It's only through everyone asking me what I've put that I've started to grow attached to it.

FORTUNA *laughs.*

ALEX   [*to the audience*] We go outside with our cups of tea and while we talk I try to work out what to say that will mean I see her again.

FORTUNA   There's my father. That's his van just pulled in next to my car. I'd better run. He'll think I've been abducted or something. You know the way fathers are.

FORTUNA *runs off.* ALEX *watches after her for a moment, then leaves.* TESSA *enters and begins setting up an ironing board.* ALEX *returns holding a small jar of honey and a note. He has not yet entered the house.*

ALEX   [*to the audience*] In the morning there is a jar of honey and a note in the mail box. 'Thanks for breakfast. F.' F. Fiona maybe?

No. One encounter, honey, a note. Is this finished for her now? Did her father say, 'Someone gave you breakfast? You'll have to pay them back. Why don't you drop over some small gift? Maybe some of that honey. And a note, something short, just to be polite.' This is all too plausible.

ALEX *enters the house.* TESSA *is ironing her blouse.*

TESSA Any mail?

ALEX Nothing. [*To the audience*] Well, I can't say there's this girl. F, I think her name is, and she had breakfast here yesterday morning and she left me some honey. My mother's far too naively optimistic for me to let her in on the matter of F. We'd both start getting our hopes up.

TESSA What will you do today?

ALEX The usual.

TESSA You've been very quiet the last day or so.

ALEX It's part of relaxing.

TESSA There's nothing wrong is there?

ALEX You'll be late. It's after eleven.

TESSA Oh God. I'm supposed to be in Noosa at twelve-thirty.

ALEX I know.

TESSA Would you mind putting this stuff away?

ALEX Sure.

TESSA *grabs her bag and car keys and heads for the back door, blouse still unbuttoned.*

TESSA   There's some of that chicken left for lunch, and some Coles salads.

ALEX   I know where the fridge is.

TESSA *smiles and leaves.* ALEX *puts a CD in the player and flops on the bean bag with a book. He is restless and can't get comfortable and has just coiled himself into a particularly bizarre position when* FORTUNA *enters.*

FORTUNA   Hello.

ALEX *leaps up, dropping the book.*

ALEX   Hi.

Both are tongue-tied for a moment.

FORTUNA   I just thought...

ALEX   I'll move this.

The ironing board is blocking the front door. The moment ALEX *touches it, it collapses.* FORTUNA *laughs.*

FORTUNA   Perhaps it needs a push start.

ALEX   It always does that. We should get it fixed.

FORTUNA *smiles.*

ALEX   A lot of very sophisticated people have done that, you know.

FORTUNA   I'm sure they have. Do you want a swim?

ALEX   A swim.

FORTUNA   I just thought I'd drop 'round 'cause I thought I'd go for a swim and the surf's much better at Kings. I didn't know if you had a car so I thought I'd drop 'round and see if you wanted to go there. [*Aware that this explanation is getting out of hand*] In case you were thinking of going for a swim.

ALEX   Yeah. That'd be good. Just let me lock up.

FORTUNA   Okay.

ALEX   What does F stand for?

FORTUNA   What does F stand for?

ALEX   Yeah, F.

FORTUNA   Lots of things I suppose. Is this a game?

ALEX   Your name. Doesn't your name begin with an F?

FORTUNA   Oh, that's right. The honey. Did I just put F? Did you like the honey?

ALEX   The honey was really nice. Thanks. And the F?

FORTUNA   Sorry, that's just a habit. Leaving notes for my family when I go out. They know what comes after F so I don't need to put the rest.

Pause.

ALEX   Okay, let's just do this the obvious way. As though we've just met. My name is Alex.

FORTUNA   And mine... mine starts with an F.

ALEX   That's all I'm getting? F?

FORTUNA   It's a good start. There are a lot of names that don't start with F.

ALEX   And I have to guess now?

FORTUNA   Nobody's making you. F might be enough for you.

ALEX You're right. Maybe I should be grateful. It would be greedy to ask for any more. Fiona.

FORTUNA [*considering it seriously*] No.

ALEX Not Fiona.

FORTUNA Not even close, Alex.

ALEX Don't say that. You shouldn't have my name. You should just have an A. An A would be tough.

FORTUNA F will be tough enough. Alex.

ALEX Fran. Frances.

FORTUNA *shakes her head.*

ALEX Can I buy another letter?

FORTUNA I'll give you another. And to show you how generous I am, I'll make it the second letter. O.

ALEX F, O. Fo... Are you making this up?

FORTUNA No.

ALEX Is it a weird name?

FORTUNA I bet you think a lot of names are weird names.

ALEX Fo. That's all I've got. Fo.

FORTUNA And the next day I see you I might give you another letter.

ALEX Okay. Is it a long name?

FORTUNA It's quite a long name.

ALEX And I get a letter a day.

FORTUNA Maybe.

ALEX Okay. Okay, Fo, I can be patient.

FORTUNA   Then let's swim.

They move to the beach and sit on their towels.
FORTUNA *has a habit of casually braiding strands of her hair as she speaks.*

FORTUNA   Is there just you and your mother?

ALEX   Yeah. Well, I have a father, but he isn't here. He's in Brisbane with his second family. I've got a step brother, Ben, who's two. I usually spend a couple of weeks up here with them each holiday, usually before Christmas, then a couple of weeks with my mother. Christmas Day is often the hand-over period, but that can be subject to negotiation.

FORTUNA   Who does the negotiating?

ALEX   Me. My mother. We have custody of me.

FORTUNA *laughs.*

ALEX   My father's pretty good about that sort of thing. He's not great about a lot of other things, but that one he's fine with. What about your family?

FORTUNA   There's my parents and my twin sisters. They're younger than me.

ALEX   What are their names?

FORTUNA   S and S. And my parents C and G.

ALEX *laughs.*

FORTUNA   Summer's pretty busy for us. It's a great time for making money off tourists. Not that we're ever out to make a lot but if we have a good summer the rest of the year's much easier.

ALEX What do you do?

FORTUNA Well, there's the honey and other things like that. And things we make.

ALEX You make money out of honey and things you make? That's wild.

FORTUNA It's not a new idea.

ALEX What do you make?

FORTUNA A few things. My father's the main maker of things. He's a potter, I suppose. My mother runs it all. My sisters and I help out when we can.

ALEX So what are you going to do now you've finished school?

FORTUNA Make things, I suppose. I haven't any definite plans. I'm pretty comfortable with all this, living here, catching a few waves when I can. I'm in no hurry to move on.

ALEX What about the future?

FORTUNA The future, like Arts-Law Queensland Uni? There are a lot of people who want to do all that stuff. I'm happy to leave it to them. And I think some of them are just doing it because people expect them to.

ALEX Yeah. Or because they're not so good at making things.

FORTUNA *laughs.*

FORTUNA Come on, show me your stuff.

ALEX The waves aren't great.

FORTUNA I know. That's why I didn't bring my board. [*She strips to her togs.*] Come on.

She runs towards the water as ALEX *strips to his Speedos.*

ALEX [*aside*] I should have worn board shorts.

He runs after her. TESSA *enters the beach house and kicks off her shoes, puts down her bag, etc.* ALEX *enters from the back.*

TESSA You'd be proud of me. Apart from lunch and coffee, I didn't spend a cent.

ALEX What went wrong? Noosa can't have run out of your size.

TESSA This was not a shopping day for Gina. 'Men are all bastards. You can't trust them.' So whatever you decide to be, for God's sake don't be a man.

ALEX You parents have such unreasonable expectations of your children. What do you want me to be when I grow up?

TESSA Don't grow. Don't even grow into your clothes. Stay young and beautiful and unspoiled.

ALEX Do you know how hard it is to get spoiled these days? I've tried. I'm the victim of rigid parenting. I'll grow up to be just like my father.

TESSA Don't make me angry.

ALEX I take no responsibility for my chromosomes.

TESSA No responsibility. You learned that from a man, right? I didn't teach you that.

LEN *appears at the door.*

LEN	How was Noosa, Tessa?
TESSA	Fine, like it always is, busy and very fond of itself.
LEN	We're having a barbie if you want to come over. There's plenty. More than Hazel and I can eat.
TESSA	That'd be lovely, Len.
LEN	I'd better keep an eye on the snags. Whenever you're ready.

LEN *crosses to a separate stage area where there is a portable barbecue.* TESSA *puts her shoes back on.*

TESSA	How was your afternoon?
ALEX	Fine. [*Pause.*] Fine. I went for a swim.
TESSA	Endless variety, these holidays provide for you, don't they?
ALEX	I'm not complaining.

They join LEN *at the barbecue.*

LEN	We've got some of those gourmet sausages from the deli. Thought we'd experiment.
TESSA	Sounds good.
LEN	Only a couple a weeks to wait, now.
ALEX	Yeah. Two weeks tonight, actually.
LEN	You're not letting it get you worried, are you?
TESSA	We're trying not to dwell on it too much. It's pretty tough all this waiting though. Isn't it, Alex?
ALEX	I'm getting used to it.

_____TESSA   Is Hazel inside?

_____LEN   Yeah, go in, go in.

TESSA *exits. Silence.*

_____LEN   So, how's your girlfriend?

_____ALEX   Girlfriend?

_____LEN   Friend of the young female persuasion. Girlfriend. The one who was over yesterday morning. The one who drove away just after we got home this afternoon. That one. Not that I'm being nosy.

ALEX *grins.*

_____LEN   You're not planning to keep her a secret, are ya?

From left: Queenie van de Zandt, Jack Heywood and Yalin Ozucelik in the 2000 La Boite Theatre production in Brisbane. (Photo: Grant Heaton)

ALEX   No. Not that she's my girlfriend, necessarily.

LEN   Not necessarily?

ALEX   I just met her.

LEN   Pretty poor timing, isn't it? Meeting a girl
        and then going back to Brisbane. Unless
        she's from Brisbane.

ALEX   No, she's from here. I want to stay up here
        a while. I don't have to go back to
        Brisbane. Not yet. My mother's going back
        though. It's a problem, maybe.

LEN   I'll have a word with her if you want. Just a
        casual mention about you staying, maybe.
        And how we'd keep an eye on you, that
        sort of thing. Would that be worth a go?

ALEX   Yeah, it might.

LEN   Does your mother know? About the girl.

ALEX   I haven't said anything yet. I just met her. I
        don't know what to say to Mum. I like this
        girl, and I just met her yesterday, so I don't
        want to go back to Brisbane yet. And that's
        not an easy thing to explain to my mother.

TESSA   [entering] Hazel wants to know if you want
        to eat out here or inside?

LEN   We might take it inside, hey? Away from
        the mozzies.

TESSA   Smells good.

LEN   Life doesn't get any better than this.

TESSA *holds a plate while* LEN *forks on sausages.*

TESSA   No, It'll be an effort to drag myself back to
        work next week.

LEN   You know, Tessa, if young Alex wanted to stay here a bit longer when you go back, Hazel and I'd be happy to keep an eye on him.

ALEX   [*nonchalantly*] That might be good.

TESSA   So how would you get back to Brisbane?

ALEX   With you if you came up for the weekend. Or on the bus if you didn't, I suppose.

TESSA   You've never been keen to catch the bus before.

ALEX   I'm not keen now. It's an option. I haven't even really thought about it. Len just mentioned it. Sounds like something to think about.

TESSA   Sure, we can think about it.

LEN   Come inside and have something to eat, mate.

TESSA *and* LEN *leave.*

ALEX   [*to the audience*] A few years ago I asked a girl for her phone number and she wrote it on my hand. My friends were impressed, and a couple of people at school even came up to have a look at my hand. I called her from a public phone on the way home from cricket practice. She said, 'I'll just check with my mother.' After a long time she came back and told me, 'My mother says I'm not ready to go out.' Okay, I said. And she said, 'Yeah. Well, 'bye then.' I thought this was unfortunate but legitimate. My friends said the long pause probably meant she had a fight with her mother because she wanted to go out with me. I liked that idea. I must have missed her emerging readiness by a matter of days, because I saw her at the movies a week later with some guy who took several opportunities to send his tongue well past her tonsils. This was not a good thing to happen to someone who was already not great at taking the initiative. I just got lucky with F. And even though I haven't seen her for two days I don't assume the worst. Normally I would. But I don't with her. This's not like me.

And as he speaks FORTUNA *is writing in the sand.*

ALEX	Fort? You're telling me Fort now?
FORTUNA	That's right.
ALEX	Fort. Like a military installation. Fort.
FORTUNA	Consider yourself lucky. I gave you two letters. I meant to come down and give you the R yesterday but I got stung by bees in the afternoon. So I stayed at home.

She shows the stings on her hand.

ALEX	Is it still sore?
FORTUNA	Yeah. Not much though. It'll be better after a swim.
ALEX	And then what?
FORTUNA	What do you mean?
ALEX	What are you doing this afternoon?

FORTUNA	Working, I suppose. Doing bee-keeper things, and other stuff.
ALEX	What are bee-keeper things?
FORTUNA	There are many secrets that can only be handed from bee-keeper to bee-keeper. I'm not sure a potential Arts-Law student should know them.
ALEX	But what if I wanted to keep bees some time? What would I have to know?
FORTUNA	It's not that easy. You'd have to start at the bottom, and the secrets come one by one, and only when the bee-keeper's ready to tell.
ALEX	So tell me about the bottom.
FORTUNA	The bottom is probably the jars.
ALEX	So what do I do with jars?
FORTUNA	Three things. Scrounge them, clean them, fill them. That's all you need to know, other than labelling, but that's separate. More advanced.
ALEX	I think I could do the jars now. I think I already have several of the skills required.
FORTUNA	Yeah? So you want to do some jars?
ALEX	Sure.
FORTUNA	Okay. This afternoon, unless you're too busy holidaying. You could do jars while I do really challenging bee-keeper things.
ALEX	Okay.
FORTUNA	So I'll pick you up at two or so?
ALEX	Good.

FORTUNA *throws a towel at* ALEX *and runs off.* TESSA *enters the house from the inside,* ALEX *comes in from outside.*

TESSA	Good surf?
ALEX	Not bad.
TESSA	Want some lunch?
ALEX	Have you got any plans for this afternoon?
TESSA	No. Why?
ALEX	I'm thinking of going out, that's all.
TESSA	Out?
ALEX	Yeah.
TESSA	Doing anything in particular?
ALEX	Helping someone with bees.
TESSA	That's very funny. Obscure, but funny. What are you really doing, or is it a secret?
ALEX	Helping someone with bees. Washing jars for the honey. They have to put the honey in jars to sell it.
TESSA	When you've washed them?
ALEX	Yes, that's right.
TESSA	Could you explain that in a way I understand? I see you sitting 'round, reading, watching cricket, swimming, all things I understand, and suddenly you're helping someone with bees. Who? And how do you know them so well that you want to go there and wash jars?
ALEX	Okay. First, just let me say there is nothing to be concerned about. It's just fine. And it's no big deal. Okay?

TESSA	Okay.
ALEX	I happen to have met someone in the last few days who keeps bees. I thought I might as well do something useful, like go 'round and help her.
TESSA	Help *her*. So this is some frail old bee-keeping woman and you're performing a good deed.
ALEX	Well, no. I have to be honest, she is not a frail old woman.
TESSA	So tell me more.
ALEX	She's closer to my age, and it's probably a big job, keeping bees.
TESSA	Forget the bees. You've met a girl?
ALEX	Well, yeah. And she's got bees.
TESSA	Tell me about her. And I don't mean tell me about her bees.
ALEX	I don't really know anything about her bees. [*Pause.*] Okay. She's just a girl. I met her on the beach a few days ago. No big deal.
TESSA	Where does she live?
ALEX	Near here. Little Mountain. Her family make things. That's about all I know.
TESSA	So exactly how did you meet her?
ALEX	She had a problem with her car. I offered to help.
TESSA	You can help people with car problems?
ALEX	No.
TESSA	It was a bold offer then.

ALEX	I had to do something.
TESSA	So what did you do?
ALEX	I brought her here to use the phone.
TESSA	Really? That's very clever.
ALEX	I gave her breakfast.
TESSA	Breakfast? She ate a meal here days ago? Why are you smiling? What did you do? What have you been doing in this house while I've been asleep?
ALEX	Don't get excited...
TESSA	You haven't...
ALEX	I haven't done anything, okay. I have done nothing that would be worth telling people. Now I think you're a bit too interested at the moment, and I think we're going to have to get you a cup of tea and calm you down, and we won't talk any more about this now.
TESSA	All right. Not another word.
ALEX	Good.
TESSA	What's her name?
ALEX	We're not talking any more about this, remember?
TESSA	Her name, just her name.

Pause.

ALEX	Okay. This is what we'll do. I'll give you the first letter of her name. And if you behave appropriately there'll be more later. And that includes being out when she arrives to pick me up.

TESSA	In her car. I can't believe I notice so little. Here I am thinking you're sitting around doing almost nothing, and all the time you're involved with a girl with a car.
ALEX	I am not involved. Okay? Not involved. Helping her with issues concerning bee-keeping this afternoon. That's all. So will you be out when she comes to pick me up at two?
TESSA	If that's what you want.
ALEX	It's definitely what I want.
TESSA	Why do you want to hide her from me?
ALEX	What I want to do is hide you from her.
TESSA	That doesn't sound like a very nice thing to say to your mother.
ALEX	Look at it from my perspective.
TESSA	What do you mean?
ALEX	Does the name Juliet mean anything to you?
TESSA	That was a beautiful story. A wonderful, sensitive story. I had to show people.
ALEX	Exactly. There'll be no more of that. Okay?
TESSA	It's okay if I get the first letter of her name.
ALEX	F.
TESSA	Fiona?
ALEX	Not even close.

The lights fade on the beach house. CLIFF *enters carrying a block of clay. He wears nothing but an old singlet.* CLIFF *leaves.* ALEX *and* FORTUNA *enter.*

FORTUNA   They were my sisters, Skye and Storm.

ALEX	What have you told them?
FORTUNA	Nothing.
ALEX	'Hi, Alex. I've got a problem with my car.' Am I dressed like a mechanic?
FORTUNA	[*laughing*] No.
ALEX	'Big's brought the *boy* home, Storm, come and see. We thought he'd be ugly the way you described him.'
FORTUNA	No self-control, my sisters, none at all. I think you should know that.
ALEX	Thank you. Earlier might have been better, but thank you.
FORTUNA	I might have mentioned the car.
ALEX	Why did she call you Big?
FORTUNA	Short for big sister. My whole family call me that.
ALEX	They never call you the F name?
FORTUNA	Never.
ALEX	I came here and I was sure someone would call you by your name.
FORTUNA	I don't think they will. I'd quite like you to call me by my name. Almost nobody does, so I'd like that.
ALEX	So are you going to tell me what it is?
FORTUNA	Yes. Come and meet my dad. My mother's out.

They move into the house. CLIFF *enters.*

FORTUNA	Dad. This is Alex.
CLIFF	Nice to meet you, Alex.

ALEX	You too...
CLIFF	Cliff.
ALEX	... Cliff.
CLIFF	I'm just airing a bit of a rash. Potter's itch, you know.
FORTUNA	Dad, you say that to everyone. Don't listen to him, Alex. This is what he always wears when he's potting.
ALEX	Even in winter?
FORTUNA	Potter's itch is just a joke for visiting yuppies.
CLIFF	Not a day for jokes, hey Big?
FORTUNA	Not for yours, Dad.

From left: Kylie Morris, Yalin Ozucelik and Jack Heywood in the 2000 La Boite Theatre production in Brisbane.
(Photo: Grant Heaton)

CLIFF	Sorry Alex. I think this must be one of those first impression things, and obviously Big wants me to create a good one. How am I doing?
ALEX	Great. I'd be lying if I said you weren't creating quite an impression.
FORTUNA	Dad, I think he's hating you. He's got this sense of humour and I think he's hating you and that's the closest he can go to saying it.
CLIFF	That's not true, is it Alex?
ALEX	No. No, not at all.
CLIFF	He likes me, Big. I can tell. It's one of those things, mutual. Take a seat, mate.

ALEX *sits on a box. He'd rather be at the dentist.*

CLIFF	So what about this place, eh?
ALEX	It's great.
CLIFF	Yeah, but what about all the development going on? What about that?
ALEX	Well, to be honest, I could probably do without it.
CLIFF	Good on you. There's only one thing worse than developers and that's people who think they're hippies. Live in the bloody hinterland and pretend they're dropping out. There's not one of them wouldn't shrivel up and die without town water. To them an alternative lifestyle means another way of making money. Maleny, Montville, all that. They're not hippies, they're wankers.

ALEX	They're only in it for the tourist dollar.
CLIFF	Exactly. Exactly. He's good this boy.
FORTUNA	Yeah Dad, I know. Is he boring you, Alex?
ALEX	No, not at all. This is fine, really good.
FORTUNA	Are you going to help me with the jars then?
ALEX	Sure.
CLIFF	Good to meet you, Alex.
ALEX	Same here.

ALEX *and* FORTUNA *move away.*

FORTUNA	You're very funny.
ALEX	Am I?
FORTUNA	Thanks for offering to wash the bottles.
ALEX	That's okay. It's interesting meeting your sisters and your father.
FORTUNA	It's all right. You don't have to be polite.
ALEX	They're interesting. Trust me.
FORTUNA	Really?

The lights come up on the beach house as ALEX *and* FORTUNA *move towards it.* TESSA *is packing to return to Brisbane as they approach.*

ALEX	I asked Skye what your name was.
FORTUNA	What did she say?
ALEX	She said, 'You'd be pretty stupid if you didn't know that. Pretty stupid if you'd come to someone's house and wash things for them if you didn't even know their name.'

FORTUNA *laughs.*

ALEX My mother's home.

FORTUNA So she does exist.

ALEX I think you should know she's not quite like your family.

They step inside.

TESSA Hello.

She inspects FORTUNA.

TESSA I'm Alex's mother.

FORTUNA Hello. I'm his friend.

TESSA I'm Tessa.

FORTUNA And I'm Fortuna.

TESSA Fortuna. That's a lovely name. Certainly not common though. It's not the sort of name you could ever guess.

FORTUNA People tend not to.

TESSA Will you stay for a drink? A cup of tea?

TESSA *picks up the kettle.*

FORTUNA No thank you. I have to get back.

ALEX Her family are expecting her.

FORTUNA Can't have Dad thinking I'm killing myself on Sugarbag Road.

TESSA Do you like Frente?

TESSA *holds up the CD that was sitting on the bench.*

FORTUNA Yeah, I don't mind some of their stuff.

TESSA   Alex's a bit of a fan, aren't you Alex? He'll wear out the CD if he plays it any more.

ALEX   CDs don't wear out, Mum.

TESSA   Silly me. Trapped in the age of vinyl.

ALEX   [to the audience] So my mother decides to make it a fairly painful experience. She can't help herself. But Fortuna seems not to mind. She laughs at my mother's jokes at my expense until she's ready to leave.

FORTUNA   Give me a ring tomorrow. If you want.

ALEX   I don't have your phone number.

FORTUNA grabs a pen from the bench and writes the number on the back of ALEX's hand.

FORTUNA   Tomorrow.

TESSA   Well, it was nice to meet you, Fortuna. Next time you'll have to stay longer.

FORTUNA   I will.

FORTUNA smiles and leaves. ALEX takes the CD from his mother's hand.

TESSA   Sorry about the Frente remark.

ALEX   I should think so.

TESSA   Why would anyone want a nose ring? How does she blow her nose?

ALEX   Mum.

TESSA   What if it got caught on something?

ALEX   Mother.

TESSA   So she is why you want to stay up here? What are you going to do here by yourself? You would be by yourself, wouldn't you? I mean, she's not going to move in, is she?

ALEX   No. I'll stay here, she might visit.

TESSA   And I'll be back next weekend.

ALEX   So it's less than a week. I'll be fine.

TESSA   And you won't do anything, will you? I mean you'll be sensible?

ALEX   I'll be as dull as I always am. Give me a break. It's like schoolies week and I survived that okay.

TESSA   I suppose so. What will I tell your grandparents?

ALEX   That I've met a girl and that's why I'm staying up here. That you think she's weird mainly because she's got a nose ring. But then to avoid panicking them you'll have to say that she seems nice really.

TESSA   That sounds likely.

ALEX   I'll be fine, don't worry.

TESSA   You will ring me if you need anything?

ALEX   Yes.

TESSA   All right. I'll see you next weekend.

She kisses him and leaves.

ALEX   [*to the audience*] I'm used to the nights here. I've been here for hundreds of them. But none when it's just me. I lie in the empty house, staring up at the dark.

LEN *enters.*

ALEX   In the morning I watch cricket with Len.

LEN   Come over for dinner later. Unless you've got plans.

ALEX   No, no plans at all.

LEN   You could invite your friend, if you like.

LEN *moves to the barbecue.*

ALEX   [*to the audience*] Next door it's the season of salads and burnt sausages. In fact I hadn't even thought of dinner. I suppose I would have worked this out at some time. It makes me wonder what else I should be planning, now that I'm here by myself.

FORTUNA *enters and joins* LEN. *It is now night.*

ALEX   At the barbecue I think I should be saying more, being more interesting, but I'm watching her.

LEN   But that was twenty years ago. It's all changed a lot now of course.

FORTUNA   Makes you wonder what it'll be like in another twenty years.

LEN   Will you be going to the markets tomorrow?

FORTUNA   Yeah, we have a stall there. My family have a stall there.

LEN   What sort of things do you sell?

FORTUNA   Honey. The twins make candles out of the beeswax. Dad sells his pottery, coffee mugs and stuff.

LEN   And what do you make?

A slightly embarrassed pause.

FORTUNA   I do this thing with old stockings and grass seed, where I put some grass seed in the stocking and stuff it with dried grass and make it into the shape of a head and put a face on it. Then people water it and the grass sprouts as hair.

ALEX *laughs.*

FORTUNA   Don't laugh, they're really popular. I get five dollars for a head, ten if I sell it with a painted jam jar for a base. You'd be surprised how many I sell.

LEN   Five bucks sounds like a bargain. Sounds like I should come and check them out.

FORTUNA   We start setting up at seven. So I probably should go.

LEN   I think we're in for a storm. Will you be all right driving home?

FORTUNA   Yeah. Thanks for the barbecue.

LEN   Those Philippine-style gourmet sausages weren't bad, were they?

ALEX   Just like they eat in Manila, I reckon.

LEN *leaves.* ALEX *and* FORTUNA *walk back to the house. Pause. Neither can think of anything to say but they don't want to say goodbye.*

ALEX   I might come to the markets tomorrow and see you.

FORTUNA   That'd be good.

ALEX   Maybe we could do something after.

FORTUNA   Yeah.

ALEX   Good. Any idea what?

FORTUNA   Whatever. I don't mind.

FORTUNA's *words are drowned out by a clap of thunder and the rain comes down.*

ALEX   You can't go home in this.

FORTUNA   No. [*She grins.*] Last summer we had storms like this just about every day. Always when I was halfway home from school on my bike.

ALEX   I caught the train. Actually, I was train prefect.

FORTUNA *laughs.*

ALEX   It seems like something long ago, school.

FORTUNA   I know. It's weird, isn't it?

ALEX   And if I ever go back there it will be different, the grass will be different and the red brick buildings, and anything even slightly the same will catch me by surprise.

FORTUNA   We moved down here when Mum got sick and I never really fitted in. There was a big surf thing happening, and I like catching waves, but I was never into it in the way the others were. I couldn't see the point. And I had my family. I always had them, wherever we moved. There was always somewhere I could just be myself. Why change into something stupid just to impress people who are stupid, so they'll like me. That's all pretty dumb I suppose.

ALEX   No, it's good you didn't change just because of other people. A lot of people would. I might. I don't know, but I might... to make people like me.

FORTUNA   Did you change to make me like you?

ALEX   Into someone who could fix a car, for example?

FORTUNA *laughs.*

ALEX   I would've had no idea what to change into.

FORTUNA   The rain's easing off.

ALEX   Yeah. [*Pause.*] What's going on with us?

FORTUNA   What do you mean?

ALEX   I just wondered, you know, well... what you thought about what's going on with us.

FORTUNA   You're very analytical, aren't you?

ALEX   Yeah.

FORTUNA   I like you. I like being with you. You're very funny, particularly when you're being serious.

ALEX   Thanks.

FORTUNA   No, I like that. You're different. And you're really nice.

ALEX   Nice? Nice is a death sentence.

FORTUNA   Not always.

FORTUNA *grabs* ALEX *and kisses him slowly and passionately.*

FORTUNA   I'd better go. While the weather's like this. [*With a suggestion that this might not be so bad*] It could get worse again and I might not be able to get home.

ALEX   My mother was worried you'd be moving in.

FORTUNA [*smiling*] I'll see you tomorrow.

ALEX *watches her leave. Pause.*

ALEX A Storm Poem:

Just us

Here

Behind the storm wall

This keeps us in

Keeps them out

Keeps them a perfect invisible distance away

Behind the bars

Of the rain.

The lights fade and then come up as ALEX *joins* CLIFF *who is holding a bottle and a glass. On the floor is a box of pottery.*

CLIFF Unfortunately it's the '93. Not the best year.

ALEX You make it every year?

CLIFF Most years, if there's enough fruit. You want to try some?

ALEX Maybe later.

CLIFF Big reckons you're going to be a lawyer.

ALEX I might not get in.

CLIFF When will you know?

ALEX Late next week.

CLIFF I went to Queensland Uni. Did Big tell you that? First six months of 1971. Great place.

ALEX You didn't stay though.

CLIFF No, wasn't the place for me. So I travelled and never got 'round to going back. Some of the people I travelled with went back. One of them even did law.

ALEX Really?

CLIFF Yeah. He came to tell me he was going to. I don't know if he was looking for me to approve, or what. As if it'd bother me if someone did law, or didn't. Anyway, the last time I saw him he was telling me the important things you can do with a law degree. That was ten or fifteen years ago. I wondered how he was going with the important things, and then I saw him on TV a couple of years ago in a pin-stripe suit, defending some white-collar criminal.

FORTUNA *enters.* CLIFF *picks up the box.*

CLIFF Another box of yuppie bait.

CLIFF *carries the box off.*

FORTUNA Come and meet Mum.

ALEX I think your father thinks I shouldn't be doing law.

FORTUNA Really, why?

ALEX He told me a story about someone who did a law degree and changed into something your father didn't like.

FORTUNA I don't think that means you shouldn't. I don't think that's necessarily him telling you you shouldn't.

ALEX Do you think it's a problem, me doing law?

FORTUNA No. Why would I? Do you have a problem with me not doing law?

ALEX Not at all.

FORTUNA Good. Good. Then no one has any problems. Did you get those plates boxed?

ALEX Yeah.

FORTUNA Good. We've got an order through for some more. We just got a fax from Lionel. He's got a gallery in Noosa.

ALEX You have a fax?

FORTUNA Yeah.

ALEX Your father has a go at yuppies and he owns a fax?

FORTUNA Cliffie will never admit to owning a fax. He hates it. In his perfect world if someone liked his plate they would give him a bag of potatoes and two chickens.

ALEX This is not easy to work out.

FORTUNA I never told you it would be easy to work out. Dad likes you. I have no idea what he thinks of your course preferences, but he...

GAIL [entering] Finally, the young man I've heard so much about.

FORTUNA Mum, this is Alex.

ALEX Pleased to meet you.

GAIL Call me Gail. We must have a chat. You can tell me the things about yourself I don't know.

FORTUNA Sit down, Mum.

GAIL   I'm fine, don't fuss. Tell Cliff dinner will be half an hour. You'll stay for dinner?

ALEX   Thank you.

FORTUNA   Mum, I'll organise it, sit down, you've been up all day. Talk to Alex.

FORTUNA *leaves.* GAIL *sits.*

GAIL   She is very important to me. [*Pause.*] Big says it's just you and your mother?

ALEX   Yeah.

GAIL   You must be very important to her then.

ALEX   Well I've never really thought about it. I suppose we're important to each other.

GAIL   I'm sure you are. [*Pause.*] We should make light conversation, shouldn't we? It's just that I think I'm trying to convince myself that you're a fit and proper person for her to spend time with. And I realise that's unfair. I can't believe I could even think of becoming that kind of parent. So just reassure me. Tell me that you don't deal drugs, molest animals, and that you won't knowingly do my daughter harm.

ALEX   All of the above.

GAIL   Well I'm glad that's out of the way.

ALEX   If you want I can provide references from teachers and lifelong family friends.

GAIL   Sorry Alex. I'm such a bloody parent, aren't I?

ALEX   So's my mother.

CLIFF	[*entering*] Alex, You're staying around for a while, aren't you?
ALEX	Yes. I think so.
CLIFF	Do you like music?
ALEX	Yes.
CLIFF	Good. Good.
FORTUNA	[*entering*] Dad, dinner in twenty minutes.
CLIFF	Do you mind if I borrow Alex for a bit?
FORTUNA	What for?
CLIFF	Thought I might take him down the back. You know.
FORTUNA	Dad.
CLIFF	He said he liked music.
FORTUNA	Have you...?
CLIFF	Alex might be the boy we've been looking for.
FORTUNA	Has he explained this yet?
ALEX	Not yet.
CLIFF	We've got a bit of a studio down there, thought you might like to see it, that's all.
ALEX	Studio as in recording studio?
FORTUNA	You don't have to go, Alex.
ALEX	No, no, I'd like to.
GAIL	Perhaps after dinner, Cliff.
CLIFF	Right. What are we having?
FORTUNA	Lentil soup.
CLIFF	Good.

CLIFF *leaves.*

ALEX   What did he mean, I might be the boy he's been looking for?

FORTUNA   You'll see. We can't let you into all our secrets at once. Can we Mum?

GAIL   You must think we're very strange, Alex.

ALEX   No, not at all.

CLIFF *returns with instruments.*

CLIFF   Where are the twins?

GAIL   They're staying over at a friend's place.

CLIFF   I didn't know that.

GAIL   Yes you did.

CLIFF   They like a bit of a sing. Do you play an instrument, mate?

ALEX   No, unfortunately.

CLIFF   Not to worry. How about... how about...?

FORTUNA   Sorry Alex. I'll take you home after this, if you want.

CLIFF *begins to play 'When Will You Fall For Me?'.*
GAIL *and* FORTUNA *sing.*

CLIFF   That was great. What did you think, Alex?

ALEX   Yeah, great. Really good.

CLIFF   [*indicating* FORTUNA] She's good, isn't she?

ALEX   Very good.

CLIFF   So, do you sing?

ALEX   Me, no.

FORTUNA   I think you might. I think you might be about to.

ALEX   No, I don't think so.

Above: Jack Heywood. Below: Kylie Morris. 2000 La Boite Theatre production in Brisbane. (Photo: Grant Heaton)

CLIFF   Just a few notes. Just lah.

ALEX   You want me to go lah.

CLIFF   Yeah.

ALEX   I don't know if I can do that.

CLIFF   Sure you can.

CLIFF *plays a couple of notes.* ALEX *lahs badly.*

CLIFF   Get yourself a bit of that wine. It'll loosen up the vocal chords.

FORTUNA   Don't do it, Alex. Better people than you have tried the lychee wine and died an awful death.

ALEX *pours himself some wine.*

ALEX   Anyone else like some?

GAIL   Doctor's orders.

FORTUNA   Absolutely not.

ALEX   This is not encouraging.

ALEX *drinks, shudders, then smiles.*

CLIFF   All right. A few more notes.

ALEX *lahs.*

CLIFF   Good.

CLIFF *plays a scale,* ALEX *lahs, gets it right.*

FORTUNA   Alex, you're fine. You're in tune.

ALEX   Really?

CLIFF   This is our boy. Do you know this?

CLIFF *plays some of 'Caravan of Love'.*

ALEX   I think so. Sounds familiar.

CLIFF   We've been waiting for the right voice to come along to sing the lead.

ALEX   Me?

FORTUNA   You don't have to do it.

CLIFF   He'll be fine. We'll have some dinner and then go down to the studio to record it. It'll be great.

FORTUNA   Dad.

CLIFF   Bring the wine with you if you wouldn't mind, mate.

CLIFF *and* GAIL *leave.*

FORTUNA   Are you okay about this?

ALEX   I don't think so.

FORTUNA *smiles and takes* ALEX's *hand and leads him away.*

END OF ACT ONE

The beach house and yard.

ALEX   [*to the audience*] This morning the toilet overflowed. I wasn't sure what to do. So I went for a swim. I walked up from the beach to the house wondering if I would be met by a tide of effluent. This didn't happen. But the toilet...

The phone rings and he answers it.

ALEX   Hello. Mum... At Fortuna's. I had dinner there. She dropped me home after... Everything's fine. Well, there's a bit of a problem with the toilet. A minor sort of overflow. Len had a look at it and he's got a plumber coming 'round soon... I wasn't trying to flush anything down there. Other than the usual. And I wasn't out all night... Everything's fine except the toilet, which would have happened anyway. I've been swimming, playing pool, all the usual...

FRED BRAHAMS *enters.*

FRED   Ya there, Mr Delaney?

ALEX   [*into the phone*] Hang on a sec, I think the plumber's here.

He puts down the phone and moves towards FRED.

ALEX   Hi.

FRED   Fred Brahams, plumber. Water closet malfunction, is it?

ALEX   What?

FRED   Your toilet. Just point me in the right direction.

ALEX   Right. Through there. I'll be with you in minute, I'm...

FRED *exits into the house.* ALEX *returns to the phone.*

ALEX   Sorry, Mum. The plumber's here now so don't worry... Sure, if there's anything, I'll ring. Okay. 'Bye.

FRED *returns as* ALEX *hangs up.*

FRED   Where are your pipes?

ALEX   Out there somewhere, maybe?

ALEX *follows* FRED *outside.*

FRED   It'll be tree roots, Mr Delaney.

ALEX   You think?

FRED   How long since they were checked?

ALEX   I don't know.

FORTUNA   [*entering*] Hi.

FRED   Afternoon, Mrs Delaney. Fred Brahams is the name.

FORTUNA   Hi. I'm not actually Mrs Delaney. I'm a friend. Of Mr Delaney's.

FRED   Ah, just friends. I'd better check around the side.

FRED *wanders off, whistling.*

FORTUNA	Who is this guy?
ALEX	The plumber.
FORTUNA	So when did we get married?
ALEX	It must have been last night. It's all a bit of a blur. Could have been a wedding. I can remember food, lychee wine, singing…
FORTUNA	You were good. Dad's been playing with the tapes all morning.
FRED	[entering, following a line] It runs along here. So what do you do for a crust, Mr Delaney? Work in Caloundra, do you?
ALEX	No, I'm a student still.

FRED *is down on the ground peering along the pipe line.*

FRED	At the university, eh? That's a good start that is. It's a good idea these days. Get yourself a ticket. University student, eh? You hear about 'em all the time. Drugs and violence and fornication. Sex is for procreation, not for entertainment. If we could all just live by that the world'd be a far, far better place.
ALEX	There certainly are a lot of problems.
FRED	And fornication's at the root of most of 'em, you mark my words.
ALEX	I'll bear that in mind.
FRED	You do that.

FRED *wanders off whistling again.* ALEX *and* FORTUNA *retreat inside laughing.*

FORTUNA	Where did you find this guy?

ALEX   Len, next door, organised it. I know he's bizarre, but at least I'll be able to flush the toilet again.

FORTUNA   He'll probably think we're in here fornicating.

ALEX   We'll have to be quiet.

FORTUNA   But what if I can't hold myself back?

FORTUNA *flops on the bean bag and begins simulating an orgasm.*

ALEX   Stop it. Please. Fortuna. Please. He'll be back in a minute.

But FORTUNA *continues.* FRED *enters.*

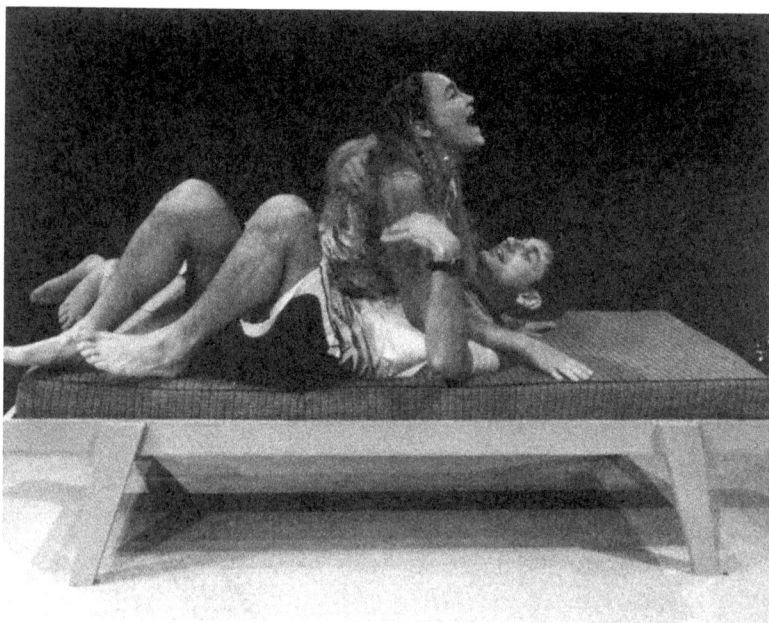

Kylie Morris and Yalin Ozucelik in the 2000 La Boite Theatre production in Brisbane. (Photo: Grant Heaton)

FRED   I've located the problem. I'll get my tools and start work. You might like to read this.

He hands ALEX *and* FORTUNA *a pamphlet.*

FRED   It's from the scriptures.

ALEX   Will it take long?

FRED   Hard to say. Pipes should be checked regularly, that way you stay out of trouble.

ALEX   Right.

FRED *leaves.*

FORTUNA   It's all about sin. You don't sin, do you, Alex?

ALEX   Hardly at all. I think I don't sin enough.

FORTUNA   Can we go for a walk?

ALEX   I should wait until he's finished.

FORTUNA   I'll be away all day tomorrow.

ALEX   What are you doing?

FORTUNA   Driving my mother to Brisbane. To see a doctor. I told you we moved here when she got sick? Well, she was actually very sick. We thought, for a while, we thought... Anyway, she's fine now. She had to have a kidney transplant, but she's okay. She had her blood tests last week, so tomorrow she has to go to the clinic. I think she'll be fine. She feels fine.

ALEX   Are you fine?

FORTUNA   I'll be better when it's over tomorrow.

FORTUNA *is about to cry. She buries her face in* ALEX's *shoulder.*

ALEX   It's good that you take her to Brisbane. She must appreciate not going by herself.

FORTUNA   She couldn't go by herself, she doesn't drive.

ALEX   Really?

FORTUNA   She says she's philosophically opposed to licensing. She made me get one, of course, and Dad's got one. I think she's just a very, very bad driver. Anyway, Dad's not good at dealing with these things, so it's better if I take her. And that's where you come in, if it's okay.

ALEX   Sure. What do I do?

FORTUNA   Just be with him. Storm and Skye won't hang around, 'cause it just makes them more worried. They'll probably come to the beach. So if you could stay with him, keep him occupied. Could you do that?

ALEX   Sure. I hope it all goes okay.

FORTUNA   Yeah.

ALEX   You're very important to them.

FORTUNA   Yeah.

They both leave. CLIFF *enters the potting studio carrying several bottles of beer.* ALEX *comes in.*

CLIFF   G'day mate.

ALEX   It's a good looking day.

CLIFF   Yeah. Look at that, out there, eh? Bloody beautiful, isn't it? One day it'll be gone. Future Urban we're zoned along here. Don't know where we'll go then. We'll sell to some bastard for some incredible amount of money and he'll put in two hundred town houses with synthetic grass tennis courts and a pool with a dolphin motif in dark tiles. It's bloody offensive. The lot of it. [*Pause.*] You want a beer?

ALEX   Sure.

CLIFF   Home brew. It's different. More like Guinness really. I don't know why though. It just worked out that way. [*Pause.*] Sometimes I get scared I'll lose her, mate. And then what would I do? This is my life, Gail, the kids. That's it. Most of the time people don't know how lucky they are. But I do. I couldn't be luckier. Gail and three glorious daughters. What a bloody life. What did I ever do to deserve it? There's no one in the world luckier than me, mate. That's why I get scared.

ALEX   She'll be all right though, won't she? It's amazing what they can do now.

CLIFF   I just love her so much. When we met there was all that free love thing going on. But when I saw her I thought, that's all I want. I just looked at her and I thought I've got to talk to that girl. And I said the stupidest things. I got myself so tense I could hardly breathe when I went up to talk to her. And she laughed. It's a hell of a laugh, mate. It only made things worse.

ALEX   Yeah. I know the feeling.

CLIFF   So you like Big?

ALEX   Yeah.

CLIFF Good. She likes you too.

ALEX Good.

CLIFF We all do. I like you. I don't think she's ever liked anyone like this before.

ALEX Anyone like me?

CLIFF No. At all. Like this. She's never been in this position.

ALEX Right.

CLIFF And you know I like you, but I'm her father, you know.

ALEX Yeah.

CLIFF And she's my daughter.

ALEX Yeah.

CLIFF And I'm not used to this, this stuff, okay? It's great it's you. I'm glad it's someone I like. That's great. You understand that, don't you? You know what I mean?

ALEX Not completely.

CLIFF Okay, okay, okay. All right, what I mean is, it's okay. Whatever... Whatever... What I mean is, it's between the two of you, okay? It's up to you. I've been through all this. I've been young. I know, okay? And whatever happens it's got to be your choice, and I'm cool, okay? Whatever the two of you decide to do, whatever you want, it's fine by me. And I think it's great.

ALEX Thanks.

CLIFF Whatever.

ALEX   You were going to show me how to make bread.

CLIFF   Sure. Sure. Just be careful, okay? You know? With the other thing? You'll be careful?

ALEX   Yeah.

A mobile phone rings in CLIFF*'s pocket He hands it to* ALEX.

CLIFF   Will you get that for me, mate? It's Gail's. Just for emergencies, you know.

ALEX   Hello. [*To* CLIFF] It's Fortuna... [*Into the phone*] I'll tell him. [*To* CLIFF] She says everything's fine. Totally fine. [*Into the phone*] Really good. We were about to make bread... Well, yeah, but he's fine... No, no. He's had a couple of beers and we're about to make bread... Yeah, of course I'll still be here. Okay. [*He puts down the phone.*] Everything's fine.

CLIFF   Good. Good. Let's make some bread.

CLIFF *leaves.* FORTUNA *enters and stands on the beach.* ALEX *watches her.*

ALEX   [*to the audience*] I think I look at this very differently from Cliff, or Len, or Mum. I can't explain it to them, any of it. I can't explain it to myself. And at any moment one of them could loom up to shout encouragement and make an awful mess of things.

As ALEX *moves to the beach, the light changes to late afternoon. He takes* FORTUNA*'s hand.*

FORTUNA I can see your house.

ALEX I wonder how long it'll be there, the way the erosion's going. We used to have more garden. I've moved in Brisbane but I thought this house would always be there. It's always seemed to me one of the inevitable things. This house and Christmas were the only things that meant my mother and my father and I had anything in common.

FORTUNA What's that like?

ALEX Parents splitting up? Better than two people who don't like each other living together. It takes a while to work out that it's better though. I don't know why. When Ben was born my father said, 'Alex, I know I've let you down. I want you to know that I know that. I'll do better this time. And I want to be there for you too, if you need me.' I said, [with contempt] 'Yeah, thanks.'

FORTUNA Do you see much of him?

ALEX Enough. More than enough. He's this weird guy who comes into my life occasionally and asks me bloke questions. Sport, girls, your future. Superannuation. It's terrifying to think that half my genes are his. It's scary enough to think the other half come from my mother. What chance have I got?

FORTUNA Your mother, has she had other relationships? Since your father?

ALEX I don't know.

FORTUNA If she did you'd know, wouldn't you?

ALEX   I guess so. So maybe that's no. Maybe she hasn't. [*Pause.*] Do you think she's focusing on me, and I'm just taking it from her? Maybe that's what's been happening and I didn't even know. She hasn't had a relationship, hasn't even tried, in case I didn't cope well.

FORTUNA   I don't know.

ALEX   Maybe I'll talk to her. Just so she knows it's fine by me.

FORTUNA   You should. My family hasn't always been the way it is. It was always okay, but I think we assumed it would always be okay. Then Mum got sick. We really thought she might die. It makes you think of things differently. You hold on much harder, when you used to just assume. [*Pause.*] I probably should get home. You want to come to Noosa tomorrow?

ALEX   Yeah. What are we doing?

FORTUNA   Taking a load in the ute. Things for galleries up there. On the way home we could go for a swim.

ALEX   What time?

FORTUNA   We have to meet Lionel at eleven. So nine-ish? We have to go the coast road. My father, this won't surprise you, my father has a philosophical opposition to toll roads, so we can't go that way.

ALEX   My mother'll be coming up in the evening.

FORTUNA   For the weekend?

ALEX   Yeah.

FORTUNA   Do I still get to see you? I mean, you should spend some time with your mother, I suppose.

ALEX   I suppose. See those trees? I used to hide under them, years ago. No one can find you in there. No one can see in. And at about this time of the day, as the sun goes down, there's this incredible light.

FORTUNA   Show me.

ALEX   Come through this side. Under here.

And they have crawled into a private world of yellow-green, dappled light.

FORTUNA   It's beautiful.

ALEX   Actually I'd really be quite happy if my mother didn't come up this weekend.

FORTUNA   You're probably not supposed to say that.

ALEX   No. But I want to spend time with you. It's like any time I'm not with you, I'm waiting until I am again.

FORTUNA   I know what you mean.

ALEX   This place is my past, my childhood. But when you're here it's different. It's as though there's a change in me. And out there you've changed the water, the sand, the whole coastline.

They kiss.

FORTUNA   I have to go home.

ALEX   All right.

FORTUNA   But I'll see you in the morning.

ALEX   Right.

FORTUNA *leaves.* ALEX *crawls out of the trees and watches after her. He moves into the beach house.*

ALEX   [*to the audience*] Sift two cups of plain flour with a teaspoon each of bicarbonate of soda, baking powder and salt. Stir in two cups of wholemeal flour and a cup of rolled oats. Beat an egg in two cups of buttermilk. Preheat the oven. Add the buttermilk and egg to the flour. Knead on a floured board until it forms a manageable but soft dough. Whatever that means. It'll take about thirty minutes in the oven. Here's one I made earlier.

He places a loaf on the bench and covers it with a tea towel.

ALEX   If I gave my mother a loaf of bread baked with all the sophistication of a house brick she would thank me and tell me it's the thought that counts. But I don't want her to settle for that. I want her to like it and to have a good weekend. I think that thought has not crossed my mind in my entire life.

TESSA   [*entering*] Hi. What's that? What's that smell?

ALEX   Bread. I've been learning to make bread.

TESSA   You have?

ALEX   From Fortuna's father.

TESSA   It smells good. It smells great. When are we going to eat it?

ALEX   When do you want to eat it?

TESSA	Well, how about for dinner? We could make some pumpkin soup. It'd be good with pumpkin soup. What do you think?
ALEX	Sure.
TESSA	I think there's a pumpkin. If you haven't eaten it.
ALEX	I haven't eaten it.
TESSA	So how was your week?
ALEX	Good, really good.
TESSA	How's Fortuna? How's all that going?

ALEX *smiles.*

TESSA	I'm your mother, I can ask these questions. You can tell me.
ALEX	It's great. We've had a great week.
TESSA	You like her then?
ALEX	Yeah. Sure. She's great. I like her a lot. Is it possible for you to keep that to yourself?
TESSA	Of course it is. Of course I can keep it to myself. What big secret have you told me anyway?
ALEX	Nothing. There aren't any big secrets to tell, but I'd still like to get back to Brisbane without everybody knowing things in advance.
TESSA	Okay. I can understand that. Are you coming back for your offer?
ALEX	I don't think so.
TESSA	Is that because you're less stressed about the result now?

ALEX   Well, I can't affect the result now. I still want it but it's not the only thing in my head anymore.

TESSA   Good. I think that's good.

ALEX   If I get Law, I do Law. If I get something else, I do that and see how it goes. Law would be good but it's not everything.

TESSA   I used to say that to you.

ALEX   I know. I didn't listen.

TESSA   You're still going to uni, aren't you?

ALEX   Yes.

TESSA   Good. You had me worried for a moment there.

Yalin Ozucelik and Queenie van de Zandt in the 2000 La Boite Theatre production in Brisbane. (Photo: Grant Heaton)

ALEX   Uni isn't everything.

TESSA   But you're still going?

ALEX   Yes, I just said it wasn't everything.

TESSA   Right. But it's a good idea. It would be a sensible thing to do.

ALEX   I know. That's why I'm doing it.

TESSA   Good.

ALEX   Everything's fine. Nothing's any different from last weekend. My plans are just the same.

TESSA   You seem different.

ALEX   I'm just the same. So stop behaving as if this is so weird. I've just been having a good time. If I told you every detail, which I'm not inclined to do because you're looking at me like I'm an alien, there is not one moment of which you would not approve.

TESSA   I'm not looking at you like you're an alien, not really.

ALEX   I'm still not telling you every detail.

TESSA   I wouldn't expect you to.

ALEX   Just the highlights. The drug taking, the nudity, the ridiculous passion.

TESSA   No. Keep it all to yourself.

ALEX   Thank you. Now, what do you want to do tomorrow? I thought we might do something.

Now TESSA *really is looking at him as if he's an alien.*

ALEX	What?
TESSA	No, that'd be lovely. Maybe we could, ah... Maybe we could go to Noosa.
ALEX	Noosa.
TESSA	Or we could do something else, what do you think?
ALEX	No, Noosa would be good.
TESSA	What's Fortuna doing tomorrow?
ALEX	Getting ready for the markets on Sunday. She'll probably come around after.

Pause.

TESSA	You don't have anything to tell me, do you?
ALEX	Like what?
TESSA	Anything important.
ALEX	Like thanks for bringing me into this world and filling my life with opportunities? What are you getting at?
TESSA	Look, tell me I'm crazy, but you know the work I do. Is this all because you have something to tell me? You're not in any trouble are you?
ALEX	What do you mean?
TESSA	Okay. I'll be specific.
ALEX	Is that possible?
TESSA	I'm not... I'm not about to become a grandmother or something, am I?
ALEX	Why do you think these things? Why can't any of this stay my business? As if it's even possible anyway. I've only just met her. You have no idea.

TESSA   You were being very nice.

ALEX   Nice? So Fortuna's pregnant, right? That's what it means when I'm nice to you?

TESSA   No. No. I appreciate it, really, now that I've got over my concerns. I just couldn't work it out.

ALEX   [*to the audience*] Fortuna turns up Saturday afternoon. I hear the Moke coming down the road. I'm ready with my towel. [*To* TESSA] I think this is Fortuna. We'll probably go for a swim.

TESSA   Don't I get to see her?

ALEX   Maybe. Maybe I'll let her come up when we get back. But please, behave.

TESSA   As if I'd say anything in front of her.

ALEX   You've embarrassed me before.

TESSA   All right, all right. Have a nice swim.

ALEX *meets* FORTUNA *as she approaches the house.*

FORTUNA   Shouldn't I talk to your mother? Just say hello?

ALEX   Later.

They move to the beach.

FORTUNA   So how was it?

ALEX   It was fine.

FORTUNA   I hope you made it nice for her.

ALEX   You'll never guess what we did. We went to Noosa. Your father's plates look good in Lionel's window.

FORTUNA	And your mother, she had a good day?
ALEX	Yeah, I think she did. Once she stopped worrying.
FORTUNA	About what?
ALEX	I was being so nice to her she thought I was in some kind of trouble. She got really tense. She even asked if you were pregnant.
FORTUNA	Pregnant?
ALEX	I've obviously never been nice to her before in my life.
FORTUNA	Pregnant? So what are we going to call the baby? Jesus?
ALEX	Do you want to go in again?
FORTUNA	No. I'd better not. I told Dad I'd only be an hour or so.
ALEX	Okay.

They shake the sand from their towels.

FORTUNA	Do I get to come in when we get back to your place?
ALEX	I suppose we can handle it. My mother does get a bit excitable though.

They move towards the house. FORTUNA *takes* ALEX's *hand.*

ALEX	Please, my mother's here.
FORTUNA	This would offend your mother? Your mother who thinks I'm pregnant will be upset by this?
ALEX	Look, I can't explain my mother. This will not offend her. She'll think it's great. She'll

think she can touch me all the time. I'd just be a lot less tense if we didn't, you know?

FORTUNA Oh, so it's your problem. What a boy.

They step into the house.

TESSA Hello Fortuna.

FORTUNA Hi.

TESSA Sit down, sit down. Would you like some tea?

FORTUNA Well...

TESSA *whips the tea towel away from a perfectly arranged plate of biscuits, tea cups, milk jug, etc.* ALEX *groans inwardly.*

FORTUNA ... sure. That'd be nice.

ALEX [*to the audience*] I knew she'd do this, do something to imply some importance. Or perhaps she thinks it's reasonable to make it look as though she's having afternoon tea catered.

TESSA So, has my boy been behaving himself, then?

ALEX [*to the audience*] Which is only one of a series of unnecessary remarks that I intend to take up with her later.

TESSA He hasn't been making a nuisance of himself?

FORTUNA He's been very sweet.

TESSA It's been nice of your family to put up with him. Your father teaching him to make bread. He made me some, it was delicious.

FORTUNA	He's been a big help.
TESSA	You're welcome here any time. You can stay for dinner if you like.
FORTUNA	I have to have an early night tonight.
TESSA	Because of the markets tomorrow?
FORTUNA	I'm really quite tired. It must be the baby.

A deadly pause.

ALEX	It's a joke. It's a joke. Because of you and your ridiculous mind.
TESSA	Alex, you weren't supposed to tell Fortuna that.
FORTUNA	I thought it was funny.
TESSA	I didn't mean to offend you.
FORTUNA	I'm not offended.
TESSA	These things do happen. I see them all the time.
FORTUNA	Is Alex always the father?
TESSA	[*laughing*] Not always. I'm sure he's very careful. I'm sure he listens to his mother.
ALEX	I think Fortuna has to go now. She has things to do.
FORTUNA	I do have to go. I told Dad I wouldn't be long.
ALEX	I'll see you at the markets.
TESSA	I'll come and buy some of that honey I've heard about.

FORTUNA *kisses* ALEX *on the cheek, mainly to embarrass him, and leaves.*

TESSA   I like that girl. She's really quite sophisticated. I was never like that when I was her age. I could never have spoken to a boy's mother that way.

ALEX   Does it bother you?

TESSA   No. No, I think I'm impressed.

ALEX *smiles.*

TESSA   And you're such a cute couple.

ALEX *cringes.* TESSA *leaves.*

ALEX   [*to the audience*] The Caloundra markets are a favourite place of my mother's, mainly because they're not actually very good. They are not contaminated by any real notion of merit. I tried to talk her out of going. I was even tempted to induce vomiting like I used to do when I didn't want to go to school. Within minutes of arriving, she's talking to Gail and Cliff like they're lifelong friends. And before I know it she's invited Fortuna's entire family over for dinner.

TESSA *enters with a clean shirt for* ALEX.

TESSA   I might invite Len and Hazel over as well, what do you think?

ALEX   Yeah, sure.

TESSA *leaves.* ALEX *changes his shirt.*

ALEX   [*to the audience*] It feels like we're just spectators. I don't fit in with this interaction. I expected that I would, you know? We're the common element. That there'd be some small talk, much of it about us and that'd be it. This feels like it has nothing to do with us.

The lights fade to night. There is music and laughter from offstage. FORTUNA *enters with glasses of wine.*

FORTUNA   It's the stuff made from grapes.

ALEX   [*smiling*] Good.

FORTUNA   Not lychees. He brought four bottles. Do you realise what four bottles would do?

ALEX   Kill four people.

FORTUNA   Probably. And home brew, he brought some of that as well.

ALEX   They seem to be getting on okay.

FORTUNA   They're an unlikely combination.

ALEX   I know. I hope it works.

FORTUNA   You don't have to play host.

ALEX   It feels like my job to make sure that long conversations don't involve at least one party being bored senseless.

FORTUNA   You think anyone's bored?

ALEX   Last time I looked Len was drinking the home brew and agreeing with Cliff on the evils of development. They sounded quite excited.

FORTUNA   Was Dad planning to write to the council?

ALEX   Yeah.

FORTUNA   He always says that.

ALEX　Gail and Hazel were comparing medical histories with some technical assistance from my mother. And they were all agreeing that men don't deal very well with illness. That's when I left.

FORTUNA　It's true.

ALEX　Skye and Storm were sitting on the grass whispering and smirking about something.

FORTUNA　So they're all fine.

ALEX　I suppose so.

FORTUNA　We can forget about them.

ALEX　I suppose so.

They look at each other with the same thought: 'Why don't they all go away and leave us alone?'. FORTUNA *puts her arms around* ALEX. CLIFF *comes in.* ALEX *is embarrassed.*

CLIFF　That Len's an interesting bloke. He's been telling me how his grandparents spent their honeymoon here. This's when it was hard to get to by road and you had to catch the boat to Military Jetty. Back when it was all unspoiled. Imagine that. It would've been paradise. And they call it progress. There was some lychee wine, do you know what happened to it?

Pause. FORTUNA *gets the bottles.*

CLIFF　What were they doing there?

FORTUNA　Mum hid them.

CLIFF　Why would she do that?

FORTUNA　I don't know.

CLIFF   Was it a joke?

FORTUNA   I think so.

CLIFF   Ah, right. I won't say a word.

FORTUNA   People might not want to drink that, you know Dad.

CLIFF   No, no. Tessa's keen to try it as an ice cream topping.

FORTUNA   She's supposed to drive back to Brisbane tonight.

TESSA *enters.*

CLIFF   The young ones are worried about you driving back to Brisbane tonight.

TESSA   Oh, I can go in the morning. I can go in the morning.

CLIFF   There you go, last of the '93.

The chorus of a Cat Stevens song begins and CLIFF *and* TESSA *sing along.* ALEX *and* FORTUNA *look at each other.*

TESSA   I'm glad I dragged out the old record player. I haven't listened to this stuff for years. And somehow it sounds better on vinyl.

CLIFF   Less sterile than on CD.

TESSA   Exactly, exactly.

CLIFF   I've got a bit of a collection, you'll have to come up and have a listen one day.

TESSA   I will. I'll do that. So what have you got, what do you like?

CLIFF Lots of Dylan, Hendrix, Cream, Credence Clearwater Revival, everything Fleetwood Mac ever did. Though 'Rumors' has got to be their best, one of the great records of all time.

TESSA Oh yes, yes, yes! I'm sure I've got it. I'm sure it's in the box.

TESSA *and* CLIFF *leave.* FORTUNA *pours more wine.*

FORTUNA Parents, what would they know about music?

ALEX My mother can be embarrassing.

FORTUNA At least she doesn't meet your friends naked except for an old singlet.

ALEX There is that to be thankful for. I have to sit down.

ALEX *takes the wine bottle and flops in the bean bag,* FORTUNA *joins him.*

ALEX I think I'm getting drunk.

FORTUNA Me too.

ALEX Where are the twins?

FORTUNA They're asleep in your room. Is that okay?

ALEX Fine. I don't think I could walk that far anyway.

They cuddle together on the bean bag and the light and noise fade slowly. When the morning sun creeps into the room ALEX *is awake and smiling as he watches* FORTUNA *sleep.* TESSA *comes in looking the worse for wear. She gets herself a glass of water and drops in two Beroccas. Seeing that* ALEX *is awake she signals him over and hands him a*

glass of water. There is a long silence as TESSA
swirls the Beroccas in the glass.

TESSA I know what happens, you know. I know
how things work, okay? And if you have
any questions, or anything, I hope you can
ask me. I hope you can feel okay about
asking me.

ALEX Yeah.

TESSA You feel okay about asking me? If you
have any questions?

ALEX At the moment I have no questions, but
I've got your number, if that happens to
change.

TESSA So have a good week, or however long
you're here. Please come home soon, or
sometime, whenever you're ready, but
hopefully fairly soon. Talk to me, phone
me sometimes and talk to me, and we'll all
be hoping that whatever's in the paper
later in the week it's okay by you. And
other than that, other than that, it's
probably important to bear in mind that
you should buy the ones with the lubricant
and the semen reservoir at the end. And
with nonoxynol-9 because you can never
be too careful. And there's no need for
anything flash, no fancy colours or ribbing
or anything. But the main thing is to make
sure it goes on early and it goes on
properly. And make sure there's room at
the tip. Okay?

ALEX	Okay.
TESSA	Good. She's great, isn't she? She's great.
ALEX	I think so.
TESSA	[*handing him fifty dollars*] This is to help with being careful. I have to go. I have to get to work.
ALEX	I'm not really happy about you driving like this. You don't look well.
TESSA	I'm fine. I'm just a bit tired, but I'll be fine.
ALEX	Call me when you get to Brisbane, okay?

TESSA *smiles, hugs him and leaves.*

ALEX	[*to the audience*] It's still early in the morning so I lie down next to Fortuna and sleep for a while until Storm jabs me in the ribs. 'You were very boring last night and you're still very boring now,' she says. 'Big only likes you because she's very boring too.' Cliff and Gail are awake by then, easing themselves cautiously into the day.
CLIFF	[*entering*] There's no hurry, is there?
ALEX	[*to the audience*] So we make tea and toast and sit on the veranda, not saying much until they decide it's time to leave.
FORTUNA	I might stay.
CLIFF	It was a good night. She's great your mother. Bloody great, isn't she?

CLIFF *leaves.*

ALEX	[*to the audience*] So now it's just the two of us and maybe the whole day, and I'm really not feeling well. My mouth tastes

like kitty litter and my teeth feel like they're wearing socks.

FORTUNA I think I need to lie down. I think I need to be somewhere not too warm and not very bright.

ALEX I'm glad you stayed.

FORTUNA Me too.

ALEX [to the audience] And we sleep with the curtains closed and the fan on until the heat of the afternoon wakes us.

FORTUNA You're not saying much. Is it the uni thing?

ALEX Yeah.

FORTUNA The offer's the day after tomorrow?

ALEX Yeah, I'd be lying if I said I wasn't thinking about it.

FORTUNA I'm getting tense for you, and I never thought I'd be tense about tertiary offers.

ALEX It's getting close.

FORTUNA Yes, it is getting close. [Pause.] Come and stay at my place tomorrow and then we'll get the paper in the morning.

ALEX That'd be good.

FORTUNA exits.

ALEX [to the audience] We go to her house in the afternoon. Cliff calls me mate a lot. Skye makes me play table tennis and she plays the way I imagine an angry Jean Claude van Damme would. I sleep on the floor in Fortuna's room. Actually I don't sleep, I sit there watching her breathe in the moonlight. In the morning we drive to the newsagent and get the paper.

FORTUNA *enters with the newspaper.*

ALEX	Am I ready for this?
FORTUNA	Get on with it.

ALEX *searches in the paper.*

FORTUNA	So, is it there?
ALEX	I'm looking.
FORTUNA	Well?
ALEX	There are a lot of Delaneys.

A long pause.

FORTUNA	Well?
ALEX	Delaney, Delaney A.P. I'm in. Arts-Law. Queensland Uni. I'm in.

FORTUNA *hugs him.* ALEX *picks up the phone.*

ALEX	Hi Mum, it's me, I didn't wake you did I...? Yeah, it's good. Thanks... Dinner on Saturday night would be good. I could catch the bus down in the morning... Of course I'll come... Yeah, it's good. See you Saturday. [*He puts the phone down.*] My mother being very excitable.
FORTUNA	Will you ring your father?
ALEX	He's probably not even home.
FORTUNA	Well, find out.
ALEX	You think?
FORTUNA	Yeah.

ALEX *punches the numbers.*

ALEX   Dad, it's me, Alex... Thanks... Yeah, it's
       good... Sure. What sort of thing? I'm going
       out with Mum on Saturday night... Sure,
       Sunday would be fine... No, it's sounds
       really good. Okay. 'Bye. [*He hangs up.*] He
       sounded excited. That is not a sound I'm
       used to, so I'm only guessing. He said he
       got the paper but didn't know if he should
       call. I get into uni and he's proud of me,
       but not game to call. [*Pause.*] I have to go
       back, the day after tomorrow. But
       Caloundra's close.

FORTUNA   Yeah, I know. Make sure you remember
          that. When you're a law student and all
          sorts of other things are happening.

The phone rings. ALEX *picks it up.*

ALEX   Hello. Dad... Uh huh... Uh huh...
       Corporate law. Yeah...? In Asia...? No. No,
       it's worth considering... I will. Okay. See
       you Sunday. [*He hangs up.*] My father
       again. Planning my future career.

FORTUNA   I want to stay with you tomorrow night. I
          have to go home soon, but I want to see
          you tomorrow and I want to be with you
          until you leave. Okay?

ALEX   Yeah, good. Stay here you mean? The two
       of us?

FORTUNA   Yeah.

ALEX   That'd be good.

FORTUNA *leaves.*

ALEX   [*to the audience*] Pass and enjoy yourself, my mother said. This is a time when you're supposed to have fun. And there *is* a small glow of satisfaction at getting into uni, but there's also a feeling that I'm being cheated of something. I feel in some ways like an unjustly condemned man planning his last day.

LEN *enters with a box.*

LEN   There's a nice bottle of wine, some wine glasses and candles. What do you reckon?

ALEX   Thanks, that's great.

LEN   You've got everything you need?

ALEX   Yes, thanks.

LEN   You sure?

ALEX   Yeah, everything's fine.

LEN *leaves.*

ALEX   [*to the audience*] For a moment I thought he was going to offer me condom money. Finally it will be just the two of us. But I still feel them all, somehow. Giving us their furious approval. Encouraging from a distance.

FORTUNA *enters. She looks different. She wears a dress for the first time.*

ALEX   Hi.

FORTUNA *holds up a toothbrush.*

FORTUNA My father said just because I was staying the night didn't mean I should forget about my dental hygiene. Where should I put my bag?

ALEX Anywhere you like, really.

FORTUNA *exits into the house.* ALEX *puts on Frente's 'Not Given Lightly'.* FORTUNA *returns.*

FORTUNA I put it beside your mother's double bed.

ALEX Okay.

FORTUNA So what's happening on the weekend?

ALEX Family stuff. Dinner tomorrow night with my mother and grandparents. Then Sunday we'll all be over at my father's. And I'm going to be nicer to him than usual, even if that's not easy. After that I suppose I'll catch up with my friends.

FORTUNA What will you tell them?

ALEX Tell them?

FORTUNA About this. About the last few weeks.

ALEX I don't know. I really don't know. I think I'd like to tell them nothing. I'd like to say it was just the same as every other year, and then listen to the lies they tell me.

FORTUNA My father, you should have seen him. Gripping onto that toothbrush and telling me about being careful.

ALEX Being careful seems to be an important topic. For him, for my mother, for Len.

FORTUNA Can we talk about that. All of that?

ALEX Sure.

FORTUNA   I want tonight to be really good. I don't want any added pressures, not that I mean pressures from you. What I mean is anything different. Anything I have to wonder about when you're gone.

ALEX   That's fine. That's good. That suits me too, really. This is good, all of this. I don't want to make any kind of mess of it. Not that I would. I don't mind letting it take time.

FORTUNA   But not forever.

ALEX   No.

FORTUNA   Soon maybe.

ALEX   Soon could be good. As long as we make sure we're careful, of course.

FORTUNA   Clean our teeth and things.

ALEX   My mother gave me fifty bucks for things.

FORTUNA   That's a lot of things. Boxes of twelve were nine-fifty in the pharmacy.

ALEX   Cheaper in Coles. I'm glad you're staying. That's what I want. Really. I want to spend every minute with you till I get on the bus. And that's the sort of thing I can't tell my friends. That's why I think I'll tell them nothing.

FORTUNA   What do you mean?

ALEX   I can't tell them what I feel, they're my mates. They'll just want to know how far I got.

FORTUNA   So what will you tell them?

ALEX   I don't know, that's a Brisbane problem. Tonight no pressures, no problems, okay?

FORTUNA   Okay.

ALEX   You hungry? I've made pumpkin soup and home-made bread.

FORTUNA   I didn't know you cooked. I didn't know you made things.

ALEX   [to the audience] We eat by the light of beeswax candles. And I can't believe she is here. I don't know how we got through that first conversation.

FORTUNA   [to the audience] We go down to the beach.

ALEX   [to the audience] Take the wine and our glasses.

FORTUNA   [to the audience] The sand is a dull silver-white and no one can see us in the dark.

ALEX   [to the audience] We go inside when it starts to get cold.

FORTUNA   [to the audience] We lock the doors and turn out the lights.

ALEX   [to the audience] I open the windows in the bedroom. We undress...

FORTUNA   [to the audience] ... each other slowly. In bed we just hold each other and fall asleep.

ALEX   [to the audience] Our heads on the same pillow.

FORTUNA   [to the audience] His breath on the back of my neck.

ALEX   [to the audience] One white sheet over us, lit up by the streetlight outside.

FORTUNA [*to the audience*] Until it's morning. Until it's time.

They move centre stage, ALEX *with a sports bag,* FORTUNA *her overnight bag.*

ALEX The bus is already here.

FORTUNA I have a couple of things for you. From Dad, the final mix of 'Caravan of Love.' And from me, a grass seed head that grows 'til it becomes a mad professor.

ALEX I wrote some poems.

FORTUNA I didn't know you wrote poetry.

ALEX That's all right.

FORTUNA *reads a little but blinks and stops.*

FORTUNA I'll read them at home.

ALEX One more thing.

FORTUNA Yes.

ALEX Can you take my library books back? I never got around to it.

FORTUNA I suppose they're overdue and I'll have to pay a fine.

ALEX I hadn't thought of that. I can pay you back from my condom budget. Soon.

FORTUNA Yeah. Soon.

The lights fade to black. 'Caravan of Love' begins to play.

THE END

Jack Heywood and Queenie van de Zandt in the 2000 La Boite
Theatre production in Brisbane. *(Photo: Grant Heaton)*

Teachers' Notes

by Nataly Redhead Beh and Collette Brennan

CONTENTS

INTRODUCTION

EXPLANATORY NOTES FOR TEACHERS

All tasks in these Teachers' Notes are directed towards use with Senior Students. Some may be adapted for use in the Junior School. **Frameworks One and Two** are designed to be implemented in the Queensland **Senior Drama Syllabus**. The activities in **Framework Three** are possible class and assessment items suitable for the **English Communication Study Area Specification** and may also be appropriately adapted for Queensland Board English (those following the 1987 Syllabus). **Framework Four** consists of possible class and assessment items suitable for the current **Trial Pilot of the new Queensland Board English Syllabus**.

ABOUT LA BOITE THEATRE

La Boite Theatre can trace its beginnings to a group of theatre enthusiasts led by Barbara Sisley and Professor J.J. Stable who formed The Brisbane Repertory Theatre. Their first production was performed on 31 July 1925. In 1967 Brisbane Repertory acquired its own site in Hale Street. At this time one of three cottages was gutted and made into a theatre-in-the-round seating between 40 and 80 people. In June 1972 *A Refined Look at Existence*, directed by Jennifer Blocksidge, opened the award-winning 200 seat theatre-in-the-round, La Boite, designed by Blair Wilson. Babette Stephens was the first director of Brisbane Repertory and Rick Billinghurst the first professional Artistic Director. In January 1993, with the appointment of Sue Rider as Artistic Director, La Boite successfully completed the transition from a pro-am theatre to a fully professional theatre company. The company is recognised for nurturing young and new artistic talent, producing new Australian works and supporting local playwrights and actors.

BACKGROUND INTERVIEWS

After January was adapted for the stage by Philip Dean from the successful novel of the same name by Nick Earls. In the following interviews both the novelist and playwright discuss the adaptation process.

INTERVIEW WITH NICK EARLS (NOVELIST)

1/ Some authors, when given the opportunity to write revised editions of their own works, choose to omit certain scenes or characters and to further develop others. If you had the opportunity to rewrite After January *are there any changes that you think you would make?*

I don't think that there are changes that I would make with many of the things that I have written from *After January* onwards. Having gone through the planning stages, got to know the characters, written the books, reworked them, gone through the editing process, seen the books come out, done the interviews, received mail from people and responded to the mail—I don't think it's productive to go back and start picking at the books and ask questions about how I might write them now. I think that my creative energy is more directed towards things that I haven't written yet.

2/ There was a criticism in the Weekend Australian *review [see p.112] that the character of Fortuna was underdeveloped. Do you have any feelings about Fortuna's character in retrospect?*

She is still written the way I would want to write her. When you choose a first person narrative you develop different characters to different degrees. You are only going to get one perspective in that 'in your head' kind of way because that's the way you are writing. I also wanted the reader to get to know Fortuna in the same way as Alex was getting to know her. I don't think that when we meet people we get to know everything about them straight up or even over a few weeks, even if we become very attached to them. I was only going to give the reader the details of Fortuna that she would give Alex and I wanted to leave aspects of her as slightly elusive. She is an object of desire for Alex, although she is real, and I wanted to make her real enough that she is believable but also not sufficiently clearly defined that everyone would read her the same way.

3/ You seem to have been working quite closely with Sarah Neal in the development of the filmscript for your adult novel Zig Zag Street, *yet you gave complete artistic control to Philip Dean to write the playscript for* After January. *Was this a challenging decision to make?*

Less challenging than I had expected. I am certainly attached to the novel but I was comfortable from the start giving over the chance to write the playscript to Philip Dean and to La Boite Theatre to stage the first theatrical version of it—because I think that they want to do it for the right kinds of reasons. Having it created and staged in Brisbane, with a playwright whose recent works have been very well received and a local theatre company, seemed like the best way for it to happen. I thought that the right thing for me to do was then to step aside and let them have a fair go at it.

4/ Robyn Sheahan, your editor for After January, *suggested in a feature article for* Viewpoint *[see p.111] that your 'central character Alex is drifting in a dream-like state, hardly aware of his destination'. Was the concept of dreams or dreaming an important issue for you when writing the novel?*

In one way it certainly was. One thing that I felt that I had to do for Alex was to suspend the real world for a few weeks. This is not like his regular life, that is how this whole thing can happen and why in some sense it is like a dream for him. Even if he is at the place where he goes every summer and expecting to do what he does every summer, it is different because this is the first and only summer of his life when he has just finished school and he doesn't know what is happening next. This guy who has been focussing hard on his potential OP score and doing all the right things at school is suddenly free to look at things a different way, to take up a different opportunity and get to know new and different people. I wanted Alex to be detached from his regular world.

5/ *In the same article, Robyn Sheahan also referred to your ability to use setting to provide 'an atmospheric backdrop to the action'. You regularly use South-East Queensland settings for your novels. Is the sense of place, which you evoke, a deliberate and important part of your writing?*

I think that stories tend to happen in a place and, to get the place right, it makes sense to use a place that you know. When using a place that you know, you find things that pose problems and in solving these problems you come up with new angles in the story. Before writing *After January* I drove around to those bits of the Sunshine Coast and stood there thinking, 'What can I see from here? What does this mean to Alex? How does it affect the way he thinks and feels?'

For years I wrote things and deliberately avoided setting them in South-East Queensland because people didn't seem to do that and the area didn't seem to be regarded as worthy of carrying a story. I was then on a Writers' Festival Panel with Andrew McGahan, in about 1993, when someone asked him about *Praise* being set in Brisbane. He said something about having read books that were set in New York and places like that where people name-dropped in such a way that they had this arrogant sense that you would understand what a place was like. That was when I first started to question the assumptions that I had been working on and started to wonder why we didn't see South-East Queensland more in fiction. I was sure it could work and I wanted to try it.

6/ *You have acknowledged that aspects of Alex, including his physique and the time that he spends in Caloundra, are autobiographically inspired. What advice could you give to aspiring young writers regarding how to use their life experiences to create works of fiction?*

Perhaps the most important thing is not to make it your diary. Biography, whether it is autobiographical or otherwise, is a different art to what I do. Much as I might have borrowed my physique for Alex Delaney, that's because it gives me something that I know. I find it useful to have some things I know there as sort of jumping-off points from which to invent.

Instead of trying to record the events of a particular time and how I might have felt and render that story as accurately as I can, what I am doing is picking up little bits here and there, things I notice or hear, thoughts that occur to me when I am out having a run or things I remember from my childhood. Things can come from anywhere and I will write them down. Often they are quite small but those are just the first building blocks of something else. There are gaps between them and I invent to fill in those gaps. Very often in inventing to fill in the gaps, you invent something more—you extend beyond it and push something in another direction and you find out new things about this evolving character who it turns out isn't you after all. So the entire process through which I create the story works on the assumption that wherever the bits come from, I am inventing the end result.

After January is in some ways a pathetic attempt at wish fulfilment. During all those years I had at the Sunshine Coast I was thinking, 'Sure, I am catching some waves, but some days the surf is flat and it's raining and there's no cricket on TV and I am bored and why do I *never* meet a girl here?'. It seemed okay about fifteen years later to finally deliver the summer holiday I wished I could have had. If only it was autobiography! That never happened to me when I was seventeen.

7/ *There have been regular rumours that you intend writing a sequel to* After January, *presumably because your readers are keen to find out what happens to Alex. Is there any possibility that you may continue his story?*

One probably should never say never but I can certainly say it is not likely at the moment. The reason is because of where I left the story poised at the end at a particular stage of Alex's journey. What I wanted to do was finish with a beginning, a chance that something might happen next, and not say whether it did or it didn't.

I did actually talk about writing a sequel before *After January* was published. At that stage I had the character still in my head and I liked the guy and I did wonder what would happen next. I made several pages of notes about how it might go when Alex went to uni. But I didn't have an answer to that and the more I thought about it, the more I realised that I didn't want to be the one to make that decision.

When *After January* came out, people developed some kind of attachment to Alex and naturally they wanted to know what happened to him. That made me even less inclined to want to say, 'Well, guess what, this is what happens next'.

INTERVIEW WITH PHILIP DEAN (PLAYWRIGHT)

1/ *You have had complete artistic control over writing the playscript for* After January. *How faithfully did you try to adhere to the original text?*

If someone asks you to adapt a specific novel, especially when it is commissioned as this was, then presumably they like the novel and its qualities and they hope that these can be brought to the stage. In this situation I think that it is my job to be as faithful as possible to the novel. In terms of artistic control, when you are writing for theatre there are always a number of practical considerations—for example, the number of actors needed because that involves expense. There are those kinds of controls which impinge right from the beginning.

2/ You wrote three full drafts of the play, After January, *before submitting it for publication. Could you try to describe some of the steps which formed the process of adapting the novel, especially how you started?*

Firstly I read the novel as a reader, forgetting that it has anything to do with me. I am just reading for enjoyment. I need to get a feel for the novel, to find bits that I like and to wonder what is going to happen next. This is a crucial reading because you only have a fresh approach once. By the second reading I will have developed some ideas and know the problems to look for, so I will read with a pencil in my hand, writing scribbles as I read. At this point I actually photocopied the entire novel, so that I had some big flat sheets to write on. This became my working copy.

3/ You have referred to practical considerations when writing for the theatre. What particular challenges does one face when adapting a novel in order to create a play?

Form

A playscript is a different thing to a novel—I sometimes think that they are even more different than people intuitively believe. A playscript is a very odd thing—it is unique in literary production. It is the only form where the relationship between what you write and what you might call 'product' is vague. When it comes to a stage play, there is no definitive production. There is a script and a production that someone might do this week but then next week, or month, or year, someone will do another production of that play with slightly different ideas so that there is never really a final product. A play is never finished, which is a strange thing from a writing point of view, because every time there is a new production there is a temptation to think, 'I might just go back and change that'.

First Person Narrative

The first problem that I had is that *After January* is a first person narrative. Someone once said of the process of adapting for the stage that 'a novel is what someone tells you happened, on stage it is what actually happens'. This is especially true when a novel is written in first person because you are getting a story told from one specific character's point of view. That is a bit tricky when you are translating to stage. You can't present one person's point of view because the characters all stand there and exist in their own right. I approached that by doing something which I would not normally want to do in an adaptation and that is that I used a narrator. The novel is told so much in the voice of Alex and he has a particular wry view of life. Lots of the little observations which he makes about himself and the world around him are comic and let us get to know him quite well. So I thought that it was appropriate to let that happen in the play and have the character of Alex speak to the audience.

Characters

The next issue is the number of characters and how you can deal with them. In a novel there can be dozens and dozens of characters who make a very brief appearance. On stage you want to confine it to a very small group of characters. This was fairly straightforward with *After January* as the novel doesn't have a huge cast.

Word Length

In moving from novel to stage you are using far fewer words. *After January* (the novel) is about two hundred pages long and this would be something like forty or fifty thousand words. A playscript is going to be sixty typed pages and about fifteen or sixteen thousand words. So you have to take out something like three-quarters of the words. Some of those words are description and you don't need to describe things on stage because people can see them. Condensing is one of the first things that you have to contend with and this obviously changes the tone of the piece. You tend to pick out the action and leave the more introspective stuff—but that can be a problem, especially if that introspection is a central part of the novel.

Time

Time in a novel is very different to time on stage. Time on stage is always real time—you can cut bits out but you can't speed things up. In a novel time doesn't really exist. You can write half a dozen sentences that bounce you across a month, a day or an hour. You can also jump backwards and forwards in time. You can't really do that on stage. You have to try to compress the meandering of time in a novel into discrete bits, called scenes.

4/ Were there any particular scenes or characters in the novel, After January, *that it seemed necessary to omit from the playscript? Similarly, were there any scenes or characters which seemed to require further development?*

There are certainly characters that were left out. It is a four-actor piece but there is doubling and tripling of roles so that there are seven characters in total. Alex, Fortuna, Tessa, Cliff, Gail, Len and Fred are the only characters that actually appear on stage. The other significant characters that it would have been fun to work with are Fortuna's twin sisters, Skye and Storm. They were cut but when I cut characters, I try to make them strong offstage characters. I like to do that when I am writing anyway, to create a sense that what is happening on stage is part of a larger world. Hopefully we will get some sense of what Skye and Storm are like as I actually have Alex using some of their lines, mimicking them.

5/ There was a criticism in the Weekend Australian *review of the novel [see p.112] that the character of Fortuna was underdeveloped. Nick Earls indicated in his interview that he remains happy with the way Fortuna was written and explained why it was necessary for him to write her that way. What are your feelings about the character of Fortuna?*

I think that Nick is right that in the novel the way her character is written is not a problem. We are only getting the point of view of Alex's character and we are seeing Fortuna through his eyes. She is a bit shadowy but that is because Alex doesn't know who she is and his finding this out is, in some ways, what the novel is all about. We get a sense at the end of the novel that maybe Alex is just beginning the process. He still doesn't know who she is, all he knows is that she is probably going to be around for long enough for him to start the process of trying to find out.

I think that the first thing that I thought when I read the novel actually was, 'What am I going to do with Fortuna?' As I said before, once on the stage the characters exist in their own right and in this situation the character of Fortuna is kind of underwritten. I worried about this for a while but I really think that it is not my job to rewrite the story, only to adapt it. I don't want to make it into my play and start thinking of things to add. I think that because I have Alex chatting away to the audience all the time, we do get a fairly strong sense that we are following him through this story and that we see

Fortuna how he sees her. All the way through the play, Alex gives these monologues to the audience. In the second last scene, when Alex and Fortuna spend the night together, I gave Fortuna some moments of speaking to the audience. This was so that these two characters kind of come together and tell us what happened. Just at that point, I didn't want only one person's view of what went on.

6/ How much contact, if any, would you expect to have with the director and/or the actors during the rehearsal process for After January?

I always make it a point to be a part of the process of production. I turn up on the first day of rehearsals and go to most of the other rehearsals. Theatre is a group activity. My script is only one part of it. A director can come along with a whole bunch of ideas and put them on top of it. Actors can come along and take the lines and say them in a way that I didn't quite envisage and do all sorts of things with them. Sitting there watching is an absolutely invaluable learning process for a scriptwriter. I also like to start talking with the director fairly early on. That, to me, is the most important collaboration.

7/ Budding playwrights often have difficulties when writing stage directions—trying to find the middle ground between incorporating too many or too few. What advice would you give to them?

Don't write too many is certainly good advice—that is usually the problem. Almost never put acting directions because actors will just hate you for it. Acting directions are those little things in brackets before a piece of text that say things like 'happily,' 'sadly,' 'cheerfully' or 'with a smile'. These make actors feel like puppets. Only put a stage direction in if you need to explain something that is actually said in the text—and remember that it probably won't be like that when someone produces it because the set design will change things. I would put in 'Walks to window', if I need that to explain why someone says, 'Hey, your car is getting towed away', when at the beginning of the scene I had both characters sitting at a table. Stage directions are really only there to make sense when you are reading the playscript. To some extent, they are not meant to be there for the actors.

FRAMEWORK ONE: IMAGINING THE FUTURE

In the play, the protagonist, Alex Delaney, is on holidays waiting for his tertiary offer and adjusting to the idea of not returning to school. In this framework students will engage in activities which encourage them to imagine the way leaving school might affect them. They will do this by picturing where they would be and what the emotional landscape might be. They will also imagine what their dream occupation might be and how close they are to achieving this. In this way they will be encouraged to use their own experiences and dreams as a way of engaging with the play when they read it.

It may be useful for teachers to read the 'Interview with Nick Earls' (which forms part of the Teachers' Notes) prior to undertaking these activities.

ACTIVITY 1.1 PICTURING PLACE AND EMOTIONAL LANDSCAPES

A. The students find a space on the floor, with pen and paper beside them, and the teacher runs a relaxation activity, concentrating on relaxing and developing their imaginative world (eg. they could physically isolate the muscles in their bodies and then think of their most relaxing places).

B. The teacher, once the students are in a meditative state, asks them to imagine that they have completed

Year 12 but do not know what they will be doing after
January. They need to think of where they would like to
be, and/or what they would like to be doing, while they
are waiting to hear the outcome of their university
applications/job applications during this break. The
teacher also reads the following quote from the novel,
After January, as stimulus:

*... the end of January is the end of the known world.
This is when I stand at the end of the known world.
This is when I stand at the edge. It's been easy till
now, relatively. I've had a new school year to face
each January, but not this year. School is over, so
there is not the usual symmetry about the holidays.
The feeling of days leading up to Christmas and New
Year and then away. Across the slow heat-heavy
weeks of January and back to school.*

*This January I'm waiting for my offer, waiting for
the code that will tell me what happens next.
Waiting.*

SOURCE: Earls, Nick.
After January, p.1

C. Once they have completed Exercise B the students are
to draw a picture of the place where they would like to
be and give it a caption that describes why it has been
chosen. On the other side of the paper they are to draw
themselves with bubbles around them describing how
they imagine they will be feeling.

D. The students then form small groups and share their
pictures. They are to choose one of the pictures to
recreate the place using freeze-frame and soundscape.
They then repeat this to show a freeze and soundscape
representing their feelings. It would be interesting to
compare how the images of place match with the images
of emotion.

E. Once the students have read the play it would be good to consider the way dreams and reality could be presented in a performance of *After January*.

ACTIVITY 1.2 DIRECTIONS

A. The teacher gathers the students and tells them s/he has incredible power and can ensure that each student in this room can be guaranteed a future in any occupation that they would really want. The students then have to think of the job that they would really like and physicalize it by finding a space in the room and creating a freeze. The teacher ensures that each student's work is observed.

B. The students then sit on the floor and the teacher tells them that his/her power has been removed and that s/he can guarantee nothing. They now need to think of their own reality (their marks, studying habits, socio-economic status, etc.) and demonstrate what they think is their most likely occupation. They then physicalize these in the space and the teacher leads the observation.

C. The teacher then leads a discussion of how the images varied and asks the students why any variations appeared and why some students didn't change. The teacher also leads a discussion to help students plan ways of ensuring they get closer to what they want.

D. Finally, the teacher asks the students to find a space and think of, and then physicalize, one very small thing they can do to get even closer to their dream occupation.

E. After the students have read the play it would be useful to lead a discussion of the dream Alex had and how his opinions of this changed in January.

FRAMEWORK TWO: LIFECYCLES

In this framework the students will be encouraged to fill in the gaps left open by the novelist and the playwright (such as what actually happens to Alex and the nature of his tertiary offer). They will also be encouraged to consider the place that leaving school plays in the lifecycle of a person. Thus they will be stimulated into imagining what life as an adult entails through their creative analysis of characters.

ACTIVITY 2.1 TOUCH AND TALK

Students are broken into pairs to represent Alex and his mother, Tessa. The pair are to represent 'the moment of truth' when Alex has the newspaper and finds out whether he was successful in his application to study Arts/Law at Queensland University. Before the commencement of any drama work the students are to decide: where they are (eg. in the car outside the newspaper offices, the lounge room); what the outcome is (ie. did he get in or not?); and finally, how their character feels about the outcome. They are to present two freeze-frames, with a brief interior monologue from each character—one before Alex shows his mother his result and one after they both know the outcome. During the presentations the teacher touches each student on the shoulder in the moment of each freeze-frame in order to hear their interior monologue.

ACTIVITY 2.2 HAND STORIES

A. The students are asked to form into groups. Each group member finishes a sentence given to them by the teacher, eg. 'When Alex began his adult life he...' (the student completes). When this is complete each student underlines the two key words from their sentence.

B. Each student comes up with a movement for each of the two key words in their sentence. They then present their sentence with the two key words and movements to the other group members. Each group member teaches the words and movements to the other group members. The teacher asks the groups to work out a sequence for the words and movements.

C. The teacher asks the groups to practise presenting the sequence in three different ways—the first time being the smallest and the third time the largest and most exaggerated.

D. The teacher asks each group to transform this into a performance sequence. They will need to consider space, levels, repetition, energy, timing and sound effects. This is presented to the class.

E. Each group reshapes according to feedback given in the presentation. These are then represented in sequential order. They may also be performed to music.

ACTIVITY 2.3 LIFECYCLES

A. The class is split into four groups. Each group is allocated one of the following four characters to consider: Alex, Fortuna, Tessa or Cliff.

B. Each small group brainstorms, on paper, four key life stages which their character experiences between the ages of 17 and 45. For Alex and Fortuna, these should begin where the play ends and develop from the given circumstances of the play. For the adult characters, these stages should show the events leading up to the circumstances at the beginning of the play.

C. The groups then devise freeze-frames for each key life stage, which they have brainstormed, along with a caption for each frame. These need to be rehearsed to ensure that the presentation between each stage is fluid.

D. Each group presents these to the class.

E. Discussion points:

- What was happening prior to the commencement of the play for the adult characters?
- How did the younger characters' lives turn out?
- What was it about the play that led us to these conclusions?
- What are the common characteristics and differences between the presentations and how do you account for these?
- How do the circumstances of the characters (social class, family structure, gender, geographical location, etc.) impact on the way that the lives of the characters evolve?

ACTIVITY 2.4 FAMILY MATTERS

Students find a partner of the same approximate size. The teacher introduces the concept of contact improvisation. This demands that the two performers stay in physical contact with one another as they create shapes. The teacher leads a discussion concerning the changing relationship experienced by Alex and his mother, Tessa, including such issues as dependency, independence and support. The teacher asks the students to use contact improvisation to demonstrate this changing relationship from a time when Alex was younger, through the current situation and into the future. The students should workshop these until they find a sequence of movements which they believe best depicts the evolving relationship. These are then presented. The follow-up discussion revolves around the depictions of the relationship as well as the effectiveness of the use of contact improvisation to create dramatic meaning.

FRAMEWORK THREE: SELLING THE NOVEL AND THE PLAY

ACTIVITY 3.1 COVER TO COVER

The choice of cover for a novel or play is an important aspect of marketing. Sometimes readers do not agree with publishers' decisions.

A reviewer of the novel *After January* warned potential readers 'not [to be] put off by a totally inappropriate and misleading cover'.

Carefully examine the cover before and then after reading the novel or play. Undertake one of the following tasks:

A. Write a letter to the publisher of the novel (University of Queensland Press) or the play (Currency Press) in which you either:
   (i) Compliment them on their choice of cover (illustrations, layout and blurb) and explain why you think it was appropriate and effective
   OR
   (ii) Constructively criticise their choice of cover (illustrations, layout and blurb) and explain why you think it was inappropriate and/or ineffective.

B. Design a new cover for the novel or play which you consider is more appropriate and effective. Ensure that you include all important information from the original cover. The wording of the blurb may be altered or maintained as you see fit.

(SOURCE: Robinson, Nicola. 'Teenage Angst Revisited' in *Weekend Australian*, 27–28 January 1996)

ACTIVITY 3.2 INFORMING THE PUBLIC

Part of the publicity campaign for most theatre companies' productions includes the creation and distribution of posters and flyers. The flyer usually consists of a reduced version of the poster on one side and more detailed information about the play and the cast on the reverse. An important feature of the flyer is a brief synopsis of the play which also appears on the reverse side.

This exercise assumes that you have read the novel and/or the play, but have not seen a theatre company poster or flyer for *After January*.

Carefully examine a flyer from a theatre company's recent production. Using this as your model, design a flyer for a new production of *After January* for that theatre company's next season. Think carefully about your target audience when making decisions about layout, choice of photo/illustration and wording of the synopsis. Remember to include relevant information regarding the cast, the director and performance dates and times.

ACTIVITY 3.3 REVIEW

After reading the novel or play, *After January*, write a review for a magazine or newspaper which is specifically aimed at a young adult market (eg. *Time Off, Dolly*). The aim of your review is to present your honest opinions of the novel or play which are framed positively and constructively. The review should encourage other young adults to read the novel or play. It is important to model the content and layout of your review on an example from your chosen newspaper or magazine.

A good review should contain some information on the characters, setting, language used and plot. You must make sure that you don't spoil any surprises for the potential reader, including not describing the ending of the novel or play. In your review it would also be best to refer to the character of Fortuna as 'the girl' or 'F'.

FRAMEWORK FOUR: INSPIRATIONS

ACTIVITY 4.1 TRANSFORMATIONS

Philip Dean was commissioned by Brisbane's La Boite Theatre to write a play based on Nick Earls' novel, *After January*. Imagine that you have been commissioned to write a play based on another young adult fiction novel. Choose the novel (in conjunction with your teacher) and write the text of one important scene from the new play.

When writing the scene, you will need to ensure that you capture the spirit of the original novel. This can be achieved through demonstrating a detailed understanding of the characters, themes and events which are central to the scene. At the same time, you should also show evidence of a development of your thinking beyond the scope of the novel as you transform the original text.

To assist you with your preparation, ask your teacher for a copy of the 'Interview with Philip Dean' (which is part of the Teachers' Notes).

ACTIVITY 4.2 SHORT STORY WRITING

Nick Earls was inspired to write his novel, *After January*, after first having written a short story entitled 'Juliet' from the perspective of the same character, Alex. (You can find this short story in the anthology entitled *Nightmares in Paradise*, pp.52–8. The character of Alex makes a reference to having written this story on pp.4–5 of the novel, *After January*.) Earls has also indicated that there are some similarities between his own personality, experiences and physical build, and those of Alex.

Develop a character which shares some of your characteristics and attributes. Write a first person short story which is narrated by that character. Be very careful to ensure that what you are writing is a fictional narrative and not personal reflective writing.

To assist you with your preparation, ask your teacher for a copy of the 'Interview with Nick Earls' (which is part of the Teachers' Notes), specifically his response to Question 6.

ACTIVITY 4.3 FEMINIST CRITIQUE

A criticism that a female reviewer directed at the novel *After January* was 'that the girl (whose secret name is part of the plot, not to be revealed here) is underdeveloped—unlike the third main character, Alex's mother [Tessa], who emerged, warts-and-all, in nosey and overprotected motherhood'.

You have been asked to write an article for the literary journal, *Viewpoint* (which is devoted to young adult fiction with a target audience of teachers, librarians and writers). In this article you are to carefully examine the female characters of *After January* from a feminist perspective. You will be required to draw conclusions regarding the messages about women which you believe are conveyed to the reader through the medium of the novel and/or the play.

If you are interested in Nick Earls' response to the criticism of the character of Fortuna, ask your teacher for a copy of the 'Interview with Nick Earls' (which is part of the Teachers' Notes), specifically his response to Question 2. It would also be helpful to request a copy of the 'Interview with Philip Dean', specifically his response to Question 4.

ACTIVITY 4.4 DECONSTRUCTING MEANING

Reviewing a play or film which has been adapted from a novel is a challenging task. Readers or viewers who are familiar with the original novel may have quite specific expectations of the adapted script, casting and final production. In such a situation, it is essential that a reviewer be familiar with the novel but also open to the new meanings which a script and production may generate.

The following exercise is confined to those students who have been fortunate enough to have seen a production of *After January* in the theatre.

Write a review for the Arts section which appears in the *Australian* newspaper each Wednesday and Friday. In this review you will need to evaluate the effectiveness of the theatre company's production of the play, taking into account the transformation process from novel to playscript to performance. (NOTE: Be aware of the challenge of distinguishing between the strengths and weaknesses of the playscript and those of the actual performance.) Ensure that in your review you make specific reference to essential aspects of performance including acting, costume and set design, lighting, sound and direction.

Ask your teacher for a copy of the 'Questionnaire/ Discussion Starter' (which is part of the Teachers' Notes) to assist you in your preparation for writing the review.

* * * * *

QUESTIONNAIRE/DISCUSSION STARTER

1. Where are the characters to be found—the setting? What significance does this place have for the play?
2. Who are the characters? What significant information are we given about them? Is there any information not included that you feel would have improved the meaning of the play?
3. What are the characters doing? Summarise the key stages of the plot.
4. Does the playwright create believable and/or interesting characters? If so, how is this achieved (consider biography, relevance, etc.)?
5. What design choices could you make to help clarify location? Would they support the play's metaphor?
6. How could specific elements of design support the fluidity between scenes and the dramatic meaning?
7. What impact could visual and verbal elements have on your engagement with a production of *After January*?
8. Could a director create physical metaphors and meaningful contact that wasn't dependent upon props? What impact could they have on your engagement with the production?
9. How could actors and acting techniques assist or not assist in engaging you with the performance? (Consider casting, vocal tone, body language, movement and relationships.)
10. How could costumes function in a performance (to show class, personality type, age, location or time period, for example)?
11. How could lighting and sound be used? What could these aspects add to a performance?

12. What is the strongest moment in this play? The weakest?

13. Overall, how successful is this play? Why?

14. *Anthropologists who look at adolescent rites of passage agree that their importance cannot be overstated, not only for the sake of the developing adolescent, but for the sake of the coherence of a society. These rituals let young people test their autonomy, learn the mores of the larger culture, and achieve the sense of mastery that alone will let them willingly leave the dependence and aimlessness of childhood behind...*

    After considering this quote from Naomi Wolf, identify the ways in which Alex moves through the rite of passage from adolescence to adulthood. Comment on his growing autonomy and his sense of mastery.

15. Do you agree with Wolf's assertion that adolescent rites of passage are not only important for the young person but also for society? Why or why not?

SOURCES:
Questions 1–13: Converse, Terry John. *Directing for the Stage*. Colorado: Meriwether, 1995.
Questions 14–15: Wolf, Naomi. *Promiscuities*. London: Chatto and Windus, 1997, p.143.

✱ ✱ ✱ ✱ ✱

BIBLIOGRAPHY/USEFUL RESOURCES

RESOURCES REFERRED TO IN TEACHERS' NOTES

Converse, Terry John. *Directing for the Stage*. Colorado: Meriwether, 1995.

Earls, Nick. *After January*. St Lucia, Queensland: University of Queensland Press, 1996.

Earls, Nick. 'Juliet' in *Nightmares in Paradise*. St Lucia, Queensland: University of Queensland Press, 1995, pp.52–8.

Robinson, Nicola. 'Teenage Angst Revisited' in *Weekend Australian*, 27–28 January 1996.

Sheahan, Robyn. '*After January* and Nick Earls' in *Viewpoint* 4.2 (1996), pp.31–3.

Time Off. (A Free S-E Queensland newspaper available every Wednesday.) http://www.timeoff.com.au

Wolf, Naomi. *Promiscuities*. London: Chatto and Windus, 1997.

ADDITIONAL USEFUL RESOURCES

Brown, Phil. 'The Doctor is Out' in *Brisbane News*, 6–12 March 1996. (Article based on an interview with Nick Earls regarding *After January*.)

Dean, Philip. *Long Gone Lonesome Cowgirls*. Sydney: Currency Press, 1996.

'Going Public' in *Brisbane News*, 10–16 February 1999. (Article based on an interview with Philip Dean regarding *First Asylum*.)

Kelly, Veronica. 'Review of John Misto's *The Shoe-Horn Sonata*, Margery Forde's *Snapshots from Home* and Philip Dean's *Long Gone Lonesome Cowgirls*' in *Australasian Drama Studies*, April 1998, pp.151–5.

Macintyre, Pam. 'Lebanese and Koori Families' in *Australian Book Review*, February/March 1996, p.56. (A review of Nick Earls' *After January* and Sophie Masson's *The Sun is Rising*.)

* * * * *

* * * * *

NATALY REDHEAD BEH

A graduate of the University of Queensland (Bachelor of Arts, 1987) and the Australian Catholic University (Graduate Diploma of Teaching, 1989), Nataly began her teaching career at Padua College, Kedron (1990). A founding member of Gyre (now CITY) Theatre (1996), she assumed the role of Education Liaison Officer in 1997. Nataly is currently the Co-ordinator of English Communication at Marist College Ashgrove (1996–).

* * * * *

COLLETTE BRENNAN

After graduating from Queensland University of Technology (QUT) in 1993 Collette completed a three-year stint at Gympie State High School as subject co-ordinator of Drama. Whilst completing her Master of Education, she has worked as a teacher of Drama and youth theatre worker in a range of community and school contexts. Recently Collette was the teacher artist on the productions of *Blurred* and *Keep Everything You Love* and also compiled Teachers' Notes for La Boite Theatre. Currently she teaches at QUT Academy of the Arts—Drama.

* * * * *